THE
PILGRIMS
—— OF ——
GREAT
BRITAIN

THE
PILGRIMS

HIC ET UBIQUE

Lord Carrington (President of the Pilgrims), HM The Queen (Patron) and Robert Worcester (Chairman) at the Pilgrims reception at St James's Palace on 22 June 1994.

THE
PILGRIMS
— OF —
GREAT BRITAIN

A Centennial History

Anne Pimlott Baker

P

PROFILE BOOKS

First published in Great Britain in 2002 by
Profile Books Ltd
58a Hatton Garden
London EC1N 8LX
www.profilebooks.co.uk

in association with
The Pilgrims of Great Britain
Allington Castle
Maidstone
Kent ME16 0NB

A CIP catalogue record for this book is available from the British Library.

ISBN 1 86197 290 3

Consultant editor: Paul Forty
Text design and layout by Robert Updegraff
Printed and bound in Great Britain by
St Edmundsbury Press, Bury St. Edmunds

This book is dedicated both to the British and American allies who lost their lives in the wars that have threatened the democratic way of life which is so important to the people of our two great nations, and to the "special relationship" which binds us.

CONTENTS

BUCKINGHAM PALACE

The Lord Carrington, KG, CH, GCMG, MC,
  President,
    The Pilgrims.

     As Patron of the Pilgrims it has given me great pleasure to support the unique contribution which the Society has made to Anglo-American relations over the years. Prince Philip and I remember the occasion of our first public engagement following our marriage in 1948 which was the Pilgrim's lunch for Eleanor Roosevelt. We have enjoyed since then a whole range of engagements with the Pilgrims which has given us the opportunity to meet many of the Officers and Members who have been privileged to belong to this special organisation.

     I congratulate the Pilgrims Society on your centenary and send good wishes to you all in your continuing role to ensure the strengthening of the many ties which bind our two nations so closely together.

Elizabeth R

January 2002

Foreword

It has been a great honour to be President of the Pilgrims Society of Great Britain for eighteen years. Particularly so for someone like myself of a wartime generation, who has reason to remember vividly the events of the Second World War and in particular the momentous day on which the Americans became our allies, after the disaster of Pearl Harbor. A day on which it became certain that we would win the war.

For those of us who took part in that, there is a special bond of friendship and shared experience which makes the relationship between our two countries so important.

The aftermath of the war, the rise to Soviet power and the creation of NATO all underline the importance of that relationship. For us, the protection and nuclear power of the United States, and for the Americans, the advantage of having a friendly and reliable ally on this side of the Atlantic.

In the changed circumstances of today, this relationship is still as important as ever it was; no one can foretell the future or what may happen in a turbulent world. We would do well to maintain our close friendship, based as it is on shared interests and values.

The Pilgrims Society of Great Britain and the United States has played a positive role in fostering, developing and cherishing that association. Many distinguished men and women of both nations have been involved in its long history. Long may they continue and long may the Society flourish.

Lord Carrington
President
August 2001

Introduction

This book has been one hundred years in the making. It stands on the shoulders of Sir Harry Brittain, one of the founders of the Pilgrims in 1902 and its first Honorary Secretary (1902–13) and Chairman from 1913 to 1919, undisputedly its principal shepherd, guide, chronicler and long-lived promoter.[1] This book has been made possible by the series of careful chairmen, secretaries, treasurers and others who have maintained box after box of carefully kept and labelled files of memorabilia such as programmes of events (some wonderfully illustrated), accounts and correspondence.

The Pilgrims who kept these records through this past century deserve tribute, and this book is just that. It is also a tribute to Anne Baker, who has these past two years been our archivist and is also – by dint of her heroic efforts digging into our past both in England and America – our biographer. She has toiled over the dusty records, been excited by discovering exchanges of correspondence between Anglo-Americans famous and obscure alike, and has set down the record of our first hundred years of Anglo-American good fellowship both in text and in illustrations. The text has also been enriched by a series of oral interviews carried out with long-serving members by Christopher Robson.

It is also a tribute to the men who founded the Pilgrims Society one hundred years ago this year. It was started by a small group of elite Londoners, both British and American, whose aim it was to gather together from time to time, whenever an excuse presented itself, to bond Britain and America. Numbering initially a few score, then quickly hundreds, and for the past few years over a thousand, the members meet to celebrate the strength of the bonds that tie our great two nations and to pay homage to the "great and the good" who play a role in keeping the "special relationship" strong.

And despite recent efforts by officials of the two nations to play down the "special relationship", the very strength of the Pilgrims, the standing of its members in both countries, the quality of the speakers at its events, all bear witness to the bonds that make the relationship special.

When Americans in that melting pot of a nation study its founding in schools across the United States, the names of English (and a few Scottish and Welsh) towns and villages feature on every page: Boston, Richmond, Bedford, Worcester, Concord, Salisbury, Philadelphia, New York, Providence, Charlestown, Cambridge, Salem, Plymouth, Portsmouth and many more. And when the founding fathers' roll is called, Englishmen lead the list: Washington, Jefferson, Adams, Hamilton, Jay and Franklin, to name but a few.

On 12 December 1947, at a dinner for General of the Armies George Marshall, then Secretary of State of the United States, Marshall distinguished between a "special relationship" and a "natural relationship", regarding the relationship between Britain and the United States as the latter, saying, 'There is no more natural relationship in international life than that between the United States and the British Commonwealth. This relationship requires no special political initiative. It is not embodied in any formal treaty or pact.'

One of the biggest Pilgrims events of the second half of the century was the Bicentennial Dinner at the Savoy Hotel in London on 6 July 1976, one of the hottest days of that hot English summer. This was before the days of air-conditioning at the Savoy, and the fans were filled with ice in an attempt to cool the room, filled to capacity (the stage had been removed to make room for more guests). The Queen Mother was the guest of honour, making her first after-dinner speech. After recalling her official visit to America in 1939, when she and the King stayed with the Roosevelts, she said, 'The Americans . . . have shared with us many years of recorded history. Their laws are based on the English Common Law. The language of the Declaration of Independence was the language of Shakespeare. And they have, in reply, Longfellow and Henry James; and it has been continually enriched by contributions from both sides of the Atlantic. These ties of culture, after some initial difficulties not unknown, endured through thick and thin until finally cemented by our shared responsibility in two world wars, in the second of which we worked together as closely as two allies have ever worked together in the past.'[2]

During the 1970s and early 1980s when the phrase "special relationship" was struck from the speeches of American diplomats, the fact of the relationship's continued existence was demonstrated by the decision of the Defense Secretary and Chairman of the Joint Chiefs, and (with no doubt at all) of the President, to provide essential intelligence and support to the British forces sent to regain the Falkland Islands from Argentine occupation. Without this assistance, it has been said, the task force might have failed. As in both world wars, America's continuing loyalty to Great Britain (in its own self-interest, to be sure), was demonstrated during the Falklands war period.

"Special" or "natural", there is no doubt that the relationship exists, and it is to the furtherance of Anglo-American good fellowship that the Pilgrims is dedicated.

This book is also a tribute to the presidents who have served it over the years, from its first president, the distinguished Field Marshal The Earl Roberts, to the eminent diplomat, scholar and historian Viscount Bryce, president during the Great War years (after his return from service as British ambassador in Washington) until 1917, when he was succeeded by Field Marshal HRH The Duke of Connaught. There followed a series of noble lords: Derby; Greenwood (briefly); Halifax, who had also served as ambassador in Washington; Birkett; Evershed; Harlech (who also had been in Washington); then that great transatlanticist, Lord Astor of Hever; and finally, since 1983, Lord Carrington, under whose presidency I have had the honour to serve as chairman. I pay tribute to Lord Carrington now for his good judgement, his willingness always to be available for counsel, for his cheerful attendance at nearly every function over nearly twenty years to meet and greet not only the principal guest but the hundreds in attendance, for his witty and wise introductions to the speakers and not least for the charm and loyal attendance of Lady Carrington at our functions.

My first function to chair was a dinner at the Mansion House hosted by the then Lord Mayor Sir Paul Newall, a fellow Pilgrim, in honour of the former Secretary of Defense (Sir) Caspar Weinberger, when 318 Pilgrims and guests filled that splendid (and just redecorated) hall, which we were told had a capacity of 312. There was a special guest at that dinner, Lady Brittain, the widow of Sir Harry Brittain, who just a few months later passed away herself. I was pleased to have been able to seat her at the head table and acknowledge her presence with us on that occasion, as she represented a link between us and those present that went back a hundred years to the founding of the Society.

I would also pay tribute here to the chairmen who have preceded me, not least to Sir Harry himself, who not only chaired the Pilgrims for six years but who supported it, encouraged others to take part in it, wrote its histories (which are the backbone of this centennial book) and who participated in its activities to the end of his days, living to be guest of honour at the Pilgrims' 70th birthday dinner in 1972.

We have had the support of Her Majesty Queen Elizabeth II, and the monarchs who have preceded her, and will have the honour of the presence of Her Majesty at a function in this centennial year. At a private lunch recently I was fortunate to be seated next to the Queen Mother, the week before her 101st birthday. Over lunch I mentioned that I was chairman of the Pilgrims. 'Oh, we attended a Pilgrims dinner in 1976,' she said brightly. 'Yes, and you were at a Pilgrims event in 1948 too,' I responded. 'We were?' 'Yes, for Eleanor Roosevelt.' 'So we were!' she recalled.

That event was a splendid occasion. On 12 April 1948, three years after the death of President Roosevelt, Mrs Roosevelt unveiled the statue in his memory on a glorious, sunny day in the presence of the King and Queen, other members of the royal family, members of the government and armed forces, and of many Pilgrims. The Royal Marines lined the route, and the service was conducted by Geoffrey Fisher, Archbishop of Canterbury and a vice-president of the Pilgrims. That evening Mrs Roosevelt was guest of honour at what was perhaps the greatest dinner in the history of the Pilgrims. Over nine hundred guests including Princess Elizabeth and the Duke of Edinburgh, in their first public appearance since their wedding in November 1947, took over the whole ground floor of the Savoy Hotel, and it was the first occasion to which members' wives and daughters were invited as guests.[3] (Fifty years later in 1998 we gathered again, British and American Pilgrims together, to commemorate and rededicate the statue of FDR.) The cost of the statue was estimated to be £40,000, and the British were invited to contribute to a maximum of five shillings per person. That the target was reached in only five days demonstrates the high regard that the people of Britain had for the late President.

There have over the years been some, though not many, changes in the operations of the Pilgrims. As noted above, women guests were admitted in 1948, 46 years after the society was founded, but not until 1974 were women invited to the formal dinners, and then only at the insistence of the wife of the American ambassador. It was finally agreed in 1977 that women should become members, and the first woman member was elected in 1978. Only in the last four decades has the practice of dining in white tie been changed to black tie.

Starting during my period as programme committee chairman (before I took over the chairmanship of the society in 1993), and continuing since then, a twice-yearly newsletter has been introduced under the editorship of Christopher Robson, twice-yearly luncheons honouring authors, junior ministers and others have been held, reintroducing the practice, from the days of Sir Harry's secretaryship, of round tables with no head table. On one occasion, in collaboration with the Anglo-American Parliamentary Group, we hosted eight visiting senators from the United States. There have been outings to places such as Kew, Greenwich and Duxford, and visits to events such as the Rembrandt exhibition at the National Gallery and a concert of American music at the Barbican. We alternate spring receptions between the terrace of the Houses of Parliament and the residence of the American ambassador in Regent's Park. The Sir Harry Brittain Memorial Lectures following the annual meetings are now regularly attended by over a hundred members, whereas only a handful had turned up before. There is now the series of Reflections lectures from distinguished contributors to our times, starting with the late Lord Sherfield, who as Sir Roger Makins had served as the British ambassador in Washington, leading up to the Reflections lecture in our centennial year, from our President, Lord Carrington.

We are pleased that there is an active American Pilgrims Society under the leadership of Henry Luce III, and that they will celebrate their centennial year in 2003.

Robert M. Worcester
Chairman
September 2001

1 See Brittain's *Pilgrim Partners: Forty Years of British-American Fellowship*, Hutchinson & Co., 1940; *Pilgrims and Pioneers: Reminiscences of Sir Harry Brittain*, Hutchinson & Co., 1945, esp. pp. 103–51; *Happy Pilgrimage: Further Reminiscences of Sir Harry Brittain*, Hutchinson & Co., 1949.
2 I have quoted this paragraph verbatim from the text by Anne Baker that follows this introduction; see p.43. [RMW]
3 This passage is also quoted from Anne Baker's text; see p.32. [RMW]

The Pilgrims Emblem. Designed in 1902 by Hugh Fisher of the Illustrated London News *following Lindsay Russell's ideas, and approved by Rider Haggard, author of* King Solomon's Mines, *the coat of arms is displayed at every Pilgrims dinner. Above the head of the medieval pilgrim is a scroll showing another ancient pilgrim gazing with amazement at a motor car, steamship, bicycle, train, and airship. The British lion is in front, with the American eagle on the back of the horse. Some subtle changes crept in during the early years, including the design of the motor car.*

A HISTORY
OF THE PILGRIMS

HE PILGRIMS SOCIETY was founded in 1902 'to promote good-will, good-fellowship, abiding friendship, and everlasting peace between the United States and Great Britain'.[1] It was by no means the first Anglo-American friendship society to be founded in England: as J. Arthur Barratt, a founder member, told General Joseph Wheeler, London was littered with the corpses of Anglo-American clubs, such as St George's Club in Hanover Square. Those that had survived included the American Society in London, started in 1895 for Americans living in Britain, for the purpose of celebrating American national holidays such as the Fourth of July and Thanksgiving Day, to which distinguished Englishmen were invited. In 1898 James Bryce, supported by Andrew Carnegie, Herbert Asquith and Arthur Balfour, helped to found the Anglo-American League, to further co-operation between the two nations. Sir Walter Besant had been aware on visiting the United States that many Americans were ignorant of British institutions, and hoped to remedy this by founding in 1900 the Atlantic Union, a society set up to entertain Americans, and British colonials, visiting England. This was aimed at the professional classes, and he hoped that by having personal contacts they might get a better knowledge of England than if they had just stayed in hotels. Many Americans welcomed these initiatives because of their growing concern at the waves of immigration into the United States from southern and eastern Europe, and their fear that the "Anglo-Saxons" would be swamped. Theodore Roosevelt, for example, distinguished between "real" Americans and "hyphenated Americans" (Italian-Americans, Irish-Americans, and so on), and Henry Cabot Lodge argued that Americans of British descent had contributed three times as much to American abilities as all the others combined. However chequered Anglo-American diplomatic relations had been in the nineteenth century, there was a strong feeling among Americans of English ancestry that the two nations shared not only a common language, but common ideals, and that there was a need to assert their Anglo-Saxon heritage. These sentiments were repeated at many early Pilgrims functions: at the first annual dinner, on 19 June 1903, Field Marshal Sir George White (governor of Gibraltar and a Boer War veteran) said that the population of the world was divided into Anglo-Saxons and foreigners, and England and America had this in common, that they were safeguarding the liberties of the people. On his return from Washington, at the dinner in his honour on 6 November 1913, James Bryce declared that the friendship of the two countries rested on 'community of language, of literature, of institutions, of traditions, of ideals, of all those memories of the past which are among the most precious possessions of the two nations'.

It was early in 1902 that several Americans living in London began discussing the idea of starting a society that would bring together Americans and Englishmen. To some extent they were inspired by the famous Clover Club of Philadelphia, which gave dinners for distinguished visitors, and by the Gridiron Club in Washington. Lindsay Russell, an American lawyer who was in London to open a branch of his law firm, Alexander and Colby, contacted several American correspondents in London, including Walter Neef, head of the Associated Press,

Lord Roberts

Milton Snyder and Albert Crockett of the *New York Herald,* I. N. Ford of the *New York Tribune,* and H. R. Chamberlain of the *New York Sun.* He then approached General Joseph ("Fighting Joe") Wheeler, who was on a visit to London. Wheeler, the famous cavalry commander in the Confederate army during the American Civil War, who reputedly had had sixteen horses shot from under him, and who more recently had fought in the Spanish-American War, in turn approached his old friend Field Marshal Lord Roberts,[2] who agreed to support the plan. Lindsay Russell invited people likely to be interested in forming an international club to a meeting at the Carlton Hotel on 11 July, and about forty turned up. General Wheeler presided, and Harry Brittain, a friend of Russell (who at that time was engaged to Brittain's youngest sister, Winifred), acted as secretary. Russell outlined the object of the club, which was international good fellowship, and plans for its organisation, and a provisional committee was appointed, consisting of General Wheeler, Lindsay Russell, Colonel Bryan Mahon,[3] Arthur Hutchinson and Harry Brittain. It was at this meeting that the name "The Pilgrims" was adopted: supposedly the idea of James Burke Roche, MP, it had nothing to do with the *Mayflower* and the Pilgrim Fathers, but was trying to express the idea that Englishmen and Americans would promote international friendship through their pilgrimages to and fro across the Atlantic.[4] Joseph Choate, the American ambassador, refused to support the idea at first because of the opposition of the American Society, but he was won over, and did attend the first dinner. It was decided to have headquarters in London and New York, and to entertain leading men in art, literature, science and public life when they came from America to England, or from England to America. They decided there was no

Joseph Choate

need for a clubhouse, as all members belonged to at least one club already, but they planned to take rooms at the Carlton Hotel in London, and at the Holland or the Waldorf in New York, and it was hoped that branches would soon be established in Paris, Berlin, Chicago and Washington. Although this was never included in the rules of the society, it was thought desirable that two-thirds of the London members should be British, and one-third American, and the qualifications for membership should be 'public service, literary and artistic achievement, journalists, men of extensive travel, and those who cross and re-cross the ocean'.[5] Membership was limited to five hundred. At a formal meeting on 24 July, chaired by General Lord Grenfell[6] (as Lord Roberts was unable to attend), Lord Roberts was appointed president, and four vice-presidents were chosen: Lord Grenfell, Senator Chauncey Depew,[7] Captain the Hon. Hedworth Lambton[8] and General Joseph Wheeler. An executive committee was set up, with the Archdeacon of London, William MacDonald Sinclair, as chairman, and Harry Brittain as secretary, and including both American and English committee members.

At the meeting on 24 July the new committee decided to take advantage of the fact that London was full of people there for the coronation of King Edward VII, and to have a great Anglo-American banquet at the Carlton Hotel to celebrate the King's recovery from his serious illness, and the postponed coronation.

In *Pilgrim Partners*, Harry Brittain tells the story of misdirected telegrams and a frantic dash round London in a hansom cab with General Wheeler, drumming up custom for this first dinner, on 8 August 1902, the evening before the coronation. In the end eighty turned up, although there were many more who were unable to come at such short notice, and they broke with age-old banqueting tradition to arrange the diners at round tables of eight, and to dispense with a top table. The idea behind this was to stimulate a feeling of good fellowship, and make group discussion easier, and the Pilgrims continued this arrangement, with if possible a member of the committee presiding at each table, to create the effect of a series of private parties, although after Harry Brittain's retirement as chairman the rectangular top table was restored.

In January 1903 the New York branch was set up, with Henry Potter, Bishop of New York, as president. It was in New York, rather than in Washington, because transatlantic passengers disembarked in New York, and it was therefore a more convenient place to hold dinners to welcome visitors to the United States. The first dinner was held at the Waldorf Astoria on 4 February, to welcome Admiral Lord Charles Beresford, close friend of King Edward VII, and later a vice-president of the American Pilgrims. Soon after this dinner, King Edward VII and President Theodore Roosevelt gave permission for the Pilgrims to couple the King and the President in a single toast, and it became the custom, immediately after the toast, for the orchestra to play a few bars of "God Save the King" and "The Star-Spangled Banner" – but the Pilgrims did *not* sing. Contacts between the British Pilgrims and those on "the other side of the pond" (this expression was already in use before the First World War) were frequent and close. Harry Brittain and George Wilson, secretary and later chairman of the American Pilgrims,[9] wrote weekly letters, one point of which was to alert each other of likely distinguished visitors. Before every function in London or New York a cable of greeting was sent, which was read out at the banquet, and from 1917 onwards the American and British Pilgrims printed pamphlets containing photographs and the speeches delivered at the dinners, and shipped copies off to the other side of the Atlantic to be distributed to all Pilgrims.

In November 1903 Harry Brittain circulated the first printed list of members. In the accompanying letter he told the Pilgrims that the club was already full with a waiting list,[10] and assured them that, although during the first year the society had been occupied in entertaining distinguished Americans in London and well-known Englishmen in New York, bringing together members on both sides of the Atlantic, they did not in future intend to limit themselves to entertainment alone. The list of members makes fascinating reading. Already the Pilgrims Society included politicians such as J. Henniker Heaton, MP, later responsible for the Anglo-American penny postage (and as founder of the Bath Club renowned for his breakfast parties after his morning swim), and Arthur Hamilton Lee, MP, ex-military attaché in

Harry Brittain

Washington and close friend of Theodore Roosevelt; aristocrats such as the Earl of Aberdeen and the Duke of Newcastle; lawyers such as the Earl of Halsbury (the Lord Chancellor) and Sir Frederick Pollock, professor of jurisprudence at the University of Oxford; and diplomats including Sir Percy Sanderson, consul-general in New York. There were newspapermen in abundance, including Charles Moberly Bell, manager of *The Times,* Arthur Pearson, founder of the *Daily Express,* Sir William Ingram, proprietor of the *Illustrated London News,* and Sir Douglas Straight, editor of the *Pall Mall Gazette.* There were soldiers – Sir W. G. Nicholson, who had served with Lord Roberts in India and South Africa – clergymen, including the Rev. Archibald Fleming, first chaplain to the Pilgrims, and writers, most notably Sir Arthur Conan Doyle, creator of Sherlock Holmes. There were also a number of businessmen, such as Sir Christopher Furness, MP, head of the Furness Line of steamers, Sir Thomas Lipton, founder of the Lipton's grocery business, Marshall Stevens, first general manager of the Manchester Ship Canal Company, John Lane, founder of the Bodley Head publishing firm, and Sir Alfred Jones, shipowner and founder of Fyffes banana import business. The American members in London were headed by the wealthy art collector Hamilton McCormick, and James Macdonald, representative of the Standard Oil Company, and also included Charles Yerkes, Chicago streetcar magnate, recently arrived in London. From the start there was a strong Canadian element: Sir Gilbert Parker, MP, novelist and organiser of the first Imperial Universities Conference in 1903, John Herbert Turner, ex-Prime Minister of British Columbia and Agent-General for British Columbia in London 1901–16, and Lord Strathcona, former High Commissioner for Canada, were all Canadians.

Despite Harry Brittain's claim that the Pilgrims did not intend to confine themselves to entertainment alone, the next ten years saw many splendid dinners and lunches, sometimes at the Carlton Hotel or Claridge's, but usually at the Savoy Hotel, especially after the opening of the new ballroom and banqueting hall (later called the Lancaster ballroom) in 1910. From its opening in 1889 the Savoy had always attracted American visitors, drawn by the prospect of American food and comforts, and other American societies in London, such as the American Society and the American Luncheon Club, always met there. During the First World War the Savoy became a centre of American activity, and it was the headquarters of the committee of Americans resident in London. Thanks to Harry Brittain's skilful use of his own contacts with the press (he was a friend of Lord Northcliffe, and organised the first Imperial Press Conference in 1909), and the number of leading newspaper editors and proprietors who were Pilgrims, every event had full press coverage. The speeches at the banquets were quoted in full in *The Times,* together with lists of the

Walter Hines Page

most illustrious guests, and full-page drawings appeared from time to time in the *Illustrated London News* and the *Daily Graphic.* London correspondents were understandably eager to secure tickets to Pilgrims functions, and in return reported that a particular event had attracted an even more glittering group of people than the last, and reinforced the Pilgrims' own assertion that they were the leading dining club in London. After the dinner to welcome Walter Hines Page as American ambassador in 1913, the *Observer* correspondent wrote: 'the after-dinner oratory of The Pilgrims is always unmatched . . . They gather at their banquet all that is best and noblest in the public life of the two great nations.' As Harry Brittain was careful always to keep prospective members on a waiting list, on the grounds that a club without a waiting list was not worth joining, its reputation grew.[11]

There were at least two dinners a year, sometimes three, and occasional lunches. The Pilgrims soon established the tradition that they should be the first to entertain the new American ambassador to Britain, and that his first official speech in England should be at this Pilgrims dinner. They also gave a send-off to each new British ambassador departing for Washington, and welcomed him back after his tour of duty. The American Pilgrims established a similar tradition. Harry Brittain and his successors were careful to reinforce this tradition at every opportunity, so that new ambassadors soon considered it *de rigueur* to make their first public appearance at a Pilgrims dinner, and made sure they arranged their social schedules accordingly. As

well as entertaining ambassadors, the Pilgrims kept a close eye on likely American visitors to London, in order to snap them up for a Pilgrims dinner.[12] When Mark Twain came to England in 1907 to receive an honorary degree from the University of Oxford, the Pilgrims were lucky to secure him for a lunch, as invitations poured in once it was known he was coming. In the days before there was a government hospitality department, the government found it very convenient to use the Pilgrims as a means of entertaining official visitors. The Pilgrims never confined themselves to

Mark Twain

Americans, but embraced all English-speaking peoples, and so were delighted to be asked to put on a banquet for the prime ministers of the Dominions, in London for the Colonial Conference in 1907, and again in 1911. If they were short of distinguished visitors, they could always entertain American embassy officials, as in 1905, when they arranged a farewell dinner for Henry Clay Evans, the American Consul-General, or great English statesmen, as in 1906, when they welcomed Lord Curzon on his arrival home from India at the end of his time as Viceroy. They did not always choose public figures, but gave lunches in 1912 for Ernest Thompson Seton, the naturalist, and Dr Wilfred Grenfell, founder of the Labrador Medical Mission.

There were some signs that all these widely reported functions had had some effect on English attitudes to the United States: for example, in the 1912 edition of *Whitaker's Almanack*, the USA was moved out of alphabetical order to a special place ahead of other foreign countries, and immediately after the countries of the British Empire. The formation of the British Peace Centenary Committee in 1911, to plan the celebration in 1914 of one hundred years of peace between the two nations, won far more support than its counterpart in the United States: when it was suggested that a statue of Queen Victoria be raised in Central Park, New York, Theodore Roosevelt warned that it would provide steady occupation for the police force in protecting it from being blown up by the Irish. But as James Bryce pointed out in his speech to the Pilgrims on his return from Washington in 1913, American attitudes to the British were friendlier than they had been.[13]

The outbreak of war against Germany in August 1914 put an end to the Pilgrims banquets, but there were several meetings in 1915 and 1916, beginning with an impassioned address by Sir Gilbert Parker, MP, on 15 April 1915, the 50th anniversary of the death of Abraham Lincoln. Sir Gilbert urged his audience to understand that Britain had the sympathy of the vast majority of the American people: 'the American government is neutral, but millions of Americans abandoned their personal neutrality from the first week of the war'. There were talks, by the writer

Lord Bryce

Hilaire Belloc on "The Present Phase of the War" on 30 June 1915; Maître Gaston de Leval, a Belgian lawyer and adviser to the US Legation in Brussels, on "Life in Belgium" on 26 January 1916; and William Hughes, Prime Minister of Australia, on "Australia and the War" on 17 March 1916. Harry Brittain also arranged for a selection of American newspapers to be laid out in a room on the ground floor of the Savoy Hotel, next to the Pilgrims office, so that Pilgrims could keep in touch with the American perspective on the war. There was one lunch, for James Montgomery Beck, Assistant Attorney-General of the United States from 1900 to 1903, on 5 July 1916. James Beck, author of *The Evidence in the Case* (1914), one of the most widely read books on the causes of the war and the reasons why Britain was fighting, and one of the leading American speakers in the cause of the Allies, came to England at the invitation of the Pilgrims. He told his audience that the Americans were loyal to the empire of English-speaking peoples, and urged them that 'the great Empire of the English-speaking race' must stand firm. After this he accompanied Harry Brittain to the battlefields of France.[14]

The United States maintained its isolationist policy through most of the war, and it was not until German submarines began to sink American ships that the American people were ready to go to war. The United States declared war on Germany on 3 April 1917, to the intense relief of the British people. American flags were hoisted over hotels, theatres, shops and private houses, and for the first time in history the British and American flags flew side by side over the House of Commons. The Pilgrims decided to welcome the American entry into the war with a banquet at the Savoy on 12 April 1917, its first banquet for three years. There were so many applications that they filled the Banqueting Hall and the

White Room, and there were still over 150 on the waiting list. The Foreign Secretary, Arthur Balfour, an old friend of Joseph Choate and himself a Pilgrim, presided. Walter Hines Page, the American ambassador, the guest of honour, told the Pilgrims that the United States had entered a European war for the first time in its history: 'we are come to save our own honour and to uphold our ideals'. Four days later, on 16 April, many Pilgrims attended the service of thanksgiving for America's entry into the war, in St Paul's Cathedral.

The American Officers' Club, at first called the Pilgrims War Club, was another of Harry Brittain's projects. He was not unaware of the publicity value to the Pilgrims of setting up a club for American officers in London. He was worried that the Pilgrims Society had been out of the public eye since the beginning of the war, and that new clubs were springing up and encroaching on the Pilgrims' membership and ideas. The American Luncheon Club, for example, met weekly in the same room that the Pilgrims had used at the Savoy, and had adopted the Pilgrims' idea of sitting around round tables, and another rival was the Empire Parliamentary Association, which entertained distinguished visitors from overseas and had begun to "annex" those from the United States. Rather than compete for leading visitors, Harry Brittain decided it was essential for the Pilgrims to strike a new line, and for the rest of the war the main activity of the British Pilgrims was concentrated on the American Officers' Club.[15] Set up under the auspices of the Pilgrims, at 9 Chesterfield Gardens, Curzon Street, the town house of Lord Leconfield, who lent it to the Pilgrims for the duration of the war, the American Officers' Club, described by the *Daily Express* as the most sumptuous club in the world, offered all the amenities of an American club, complete with an American bar, to all American

Prince Arthur,
Duke of Connaught

army and navy officers in London. Seen as a gift from the British to the Americans, the club levied no subscription from the American officers, who were automatically members, and all Pilgrims were encouraged to join – and most did – at an annual subscription of £5 a year, and to lunch and dine there regularly. The club, run by an executive committee chaired by Harry Brittain, with the help of John Wilson Taylor, chairman of the house committee, opened on 24 October 1917, with its official opening by the Duke of Connaught on 20 November. There was an informal dinner every Thursday, sometimes accompanied by a talk by a Cabinet minister such as the Foreign Secretary, Arthur Balfour, or the Secretary of State for War, Lord Derby, or a British army or naval officer, including the First Sea Lord, Admiral Sir Rosslyn Wemyss, and General Sir William Robertson, Chief of the Imperial General Staff. At some of the Thursday dinners there was a smoking concert – these proved more popular than the lectures. A Ladies' Committee arranged invitations to weekend house parties, twenty golf clubs offered membership, and Harry Brittain even organised an Anglo-American Christmas Holiday Party on 14 January 1919, so that the American officers could meet some English children: the entire cast of *Peter Pan* provided some of the entertainment, and by special permission of the Home Office, real ice cream was served.[16]

After the war ended, the Pilgrims held a Thanksgiving Day lunch on 28 November 1918 to 'give thanks for the wondrous co-operation existing between our two nations today – a co-operation for which the Pilgrims on either side of the Atlantic have worked for more than sixteen years past'.[17] The American Officers' Club closed its doors on 14 May 1919, after the last American officer had gone home. New ideas were in the air about the future direction of the Pilgrims, and there was a feeling that it should be more than just a dining club. The success of the American Officers' Club had prompted some Pilgrims to broach the idea of a permanent clubhouse in London, which would be a headquarters of Anglo-American friendship and would attract visiting Americans, who would stay there in preference to a hotel. Others wanted to extend branches to other cities, and a Liverpool committee was established in January 1919 with John Sandeman Allen as chairman, in order to look after well-known Americans arriving at or leaving from Liverpool, but its existence was brief. The Pilgrims were very much aware of rival Anglo-American societies appearing on the scene,[18] such as the American Club, established in Piccadilly in 1918 for Americans resident in London. The biggest threat seemed to come from the English-Speaking Union, started in 1918 by Evelyn Wrench, founder of the Overseas League. The ESU stated its aim to be 'to draw together in the bond of comradeship the English-speaking peoples of the World'. It had a clubhouse in London and a sister society in New York, and the English president was ex-prime minister Arthur Balfour (a Pilgrim), with the former president of the United States, William Taft, as his opposite number in New York. Already in August 1919 Wrench was writing to Lady Randolph Churchill that the English-Speaking Union was the strongest Anglo-American society in existence, with branches rapidly being established throughout Britain and the United States, and he was anxious to enrol everyone who believed that the future of the world depended on Anglo-American friendship.

Meanwhile, Harry Brittain had been knighted in June 1918, and elected Conservative MP for Acton in the general election of December 1918. Deciding that he could no longer devote enough time to the Pilgrims, he announced his intention of retiring as chairman.[19] William Henry Grenfell, 1st Baron Desborough, was elected chairman in October 1919, and John Wilson Taylor became honorary secretary, the beginning of a very different era in the history of the Pilgrims. Desborough and Wilson Taylor were an ideal combination: they had worked together as president and secretary of the Bath Club for years, and complemented each other perfectly. Lord Desborough was a famous sportsman,

Lord Desborough

sociable and charming, who enjoyed presiding at Pilgrims dinners, but he was also conscientious, and had the ideals of the Pilgrims very much at heart. John Wilson Taylor was quiet and kindly,[20] meticulous and very efficient, keeping out of the limelight, but rarely missing an opportunity to snap up an important American visitor to Britain.[21] Although the immediate postwar years were a difficult period in Anglo-American diplomatic relations, the Pilgrims soon settled down to their traditional activity of organising sumptuous dinners, and the ideas aired in 1918 and 1919 were quietly forgotten. There was, in fact, a lot of co-operation between

*The Prince of Wales,
later Edward VIII*

the Anglo-American societies in London, and by 1921 most of their officers were also Pilgrims.[22] J. Wilson Taylor tried to maintain the superiority of the Pilgrims by asserting their right to be the first to welcome the American ambassador and others,[23] and he was delighted to have beaten all his rivals in securing the Prince of Wales for a dinner on his return from America in 1920.[24] While there continued to be extensive press coverage of Pilgrims events, the speeches at the dinners reached an even wider audience when the BBC began live broadcasts

John Wilson Taylor

from Pilgrims dinners. This seems to have been a BBC initiative,[25] and the first broadcast was on 6 March 1924, on the occasion of the dinner to welcome Sir Auckland Geddes home from Washington. The three main speeches, given by Stanley Baldwin, MP, John Robert Clynes, MP, and Sir Auckland Geddes went out over the air, and this was clearly a success, as from then on the speeches at Pilgrims dinners were broadcast regularly. Whenever the names of politicians appeared on the list of speakers, the BBC had to check in advance that there would be no political references at the dinner, as under Post Office regulations these were not allowed, but Wilson Taylor was able to reassure them that 'the Pilgrims have no politics'.[26] A few years later, in 1930, Paramount Sound News asked permission to film the banquet given on 28 January for the delegates to the London Naval Conference. After much discussion with the Foreign Office, they were allowed to go ahead, and it appeared on British Movietone News newsreels in cinemas throughout the British Isles the following week, and was expected to be seen by forty million people in the United States.[27] There were a lot of complaints about the glare of the spotlights and the noise, and also several Pilgrims were worried that the filming would destroy the intimate character of the dinners, and interfere with the freedom of speech. Similar worries were to prevent the televising of dinners in the 1950s.

The list of functions during the Desborough years – he chaired 57 altogether – looks impressive, but behind the scenes John Wilson Taylor was constantly worrying about getting the right sort of speaker, and maintaining the high standard of the dinners. When relations between the two countries were difficult, sometimes the supply of speakers dried up altogether.[28] As well as the traditional banquets for the British and American ambassadors, important functions included dinners for the Chancellor of the Exchequer, Stanley Baldwin, in 1923, the Duke of York in 1926, the Viceroy of India from 1921 to 1926, Lord Reading, in 1926, and the Governor General of the Irish Free State, Timothy Healy, in 1928. Distinguished American guests included the Chief Justice of the Supreme Court and ex-President of the United States William Taft, who told Pilgrims at the dinner on 22 April 1922 that since the war the United States had been going through a period of convalescence, and that membership of the League of Nations would have had to overcome a deep-seated desire to keep out of European entanglements.[29]

Lord Desborough particularly enjoyed presiding at the many sporting functions, including dinners for the Cornell University cross-country team in 1920, and the United States polo team in 1921, and a lunch for the Columbia University rowing team, which had come over to compete at Henley; guests at this lunch included members of the Oxford and Cambridge University boat clubs. Rather different from these dinners for teams from Ivy League colleges were the dinners in 1926 and 1929 for the football team from Worcester, Massachusetts. This was not American football but soccer, and the visiting amateur team played a series of matches organised by the Worcestershire Sports Fellowship, which arranged sporting contests between Worcester, England, and Worcester, USA.[30]

Sometimes the Pilgrims entertained groups of visiting Americans, as in June 1925, when they put on a dinner for Dr Charles Mayo, of the Mayo Institute, and representatives of the five hundred American doctors from the Inter-State Post Graduate Assembly of America. Fifty British and American doctors were invited as official guests, while a hundred more American doctors were invited as guests by individual members. They also had a long tradition of honouring scholars, especially presidents of American universities, as when they gave a lunch in April 1922 for Dr Arthur Hadley, President Emeritus of Yale, and in October 1925 they entertained Dr Robert McElroy, Harmsworth Professor of American History at the University of Oxford, and Professor of American History at Princeton. The guest list for this lunch included an impressive line-up of historians, including A. F. Pollard (Professor of History, London University), Professor H. W. C. Davis (Professor of Modern History, Manchester University), and Sir Charles Oman (Chichele Professor of Modern History, Oxford University), and the vice-chancellors of the universities of Oxford and London. When the Rhodes Trust announced the endowment of a Rhodes Memorial Lectureship in June 1926, Wilson Taylor was quick off the mark in writing to Sir Otto Beit the day it was announced, suggesting that the Pilgrims should be the first to entertain the new fellow (provided it was not a woman!). The Rhodes trustees approved this suggestion in principle, although they wrote to the first Rhodes lecturer, Sir Robert Borden (Prime Minister of Canada 1911–20), to say that it was up to him whether he accepted. Borden came to England for the summer term of 1927, and the Pilgrims duly organised a dinner for him on 18 May. The Rhodes lectures lasted only until 1936, and there were no further overtures from the Pilgrims.

Lord Desborough resigned as chairman in 1929, and was succeeded by Edward Stanley, 17th Earl of Derby, who had been Secretary of State for War from 1916 to 1918. John Wilson Taylor remained as honorary secretary, and died in office in 1943. Although he was upset at the resignation of Lord Desborough, feeling that there had been a friendliness between the chairman and the members of the Pilgrims which was rare in most organisations, he welcomed Lord Derby as

Lord Derby

chairman.[31] Lord Derby took on the post on the understanding that it would not take up much of his time: he spent most of his time at Knowsley, his country seat in Lancashire, where he busied himself with local affairs and devoted himself to his passion for racing,[32] spent every winter in Cannes, and went to North Wales every summer for his cure. In view of this, the Pilgrims appointed a vice-chairman, Lord Hewart, the Lord Chief Justice. Although he did not preside at any functions, Lord Hewart was usually in London and could chair committee meetings. Wilson Taylor wrote Lord Derby's speeches, and even included stage directions: in the speech for the farewell lunch for Albert Halstead, the US Consul-General, after a remark about ambassadors not having to retire at 65 there is a note that says 'turn to Mr Mellon'. Lord Derby was there for all the important functions, presiding at 27 during his sixteen-year chairmanship, but he pursued a policy of not giving dinners for the sake of giving dinners, feeling it was preferable to have long gaps between functions.[33] There continued to be gaps when the political situation was tricky: for example, there was nothing between the lunch for Cordell Hull, the Secretary of State of the United States, and the delegates to the Monetary and Economic Conference, in June 1933, and the lunch for Cass Gilbert, the American artist, in May 1934.

The Pilgrims were by now well established, and no big changes accompanied the change in chairman. J. Wilson Taylor kept a tight rein on the membership, and although according to the rules of the society there could be up to 750 members, he limited it to 600.[34] He also tried to keep the society free of politics, and after the lunch on 26 November 1936 for James Farley, Postmaster-General of the United

States, just after the presidential election, he sent a transcript of Farley's speech to the ambassador, asking his advice as to whether he should omit a section which seemed to have some political bias when he had the speeches printed.[35] The Pilgrims were working more and more closely with the Foreign Office, and the number of MPs who were Pilgrims had grown from eight in 1913 to 27 in 1928. When the Pilgrims gave a dinner for the delegates to the London Naval Conference in 1930, the Prime Minister actually selected 28 January as the date, and at the dinner the Foreign Secretary, Arthur Henderson, stressed the value of such dinners: 'The Pilgrims are an organisation of better relations between the nations of the world. No one can estimate what they have done to remove and smooth away the difficulties and misunderstandings between the Anglo-Saxon peoples.' After the lunch for the delegates to the Monetary Conference in 1933, William Ormsby Gore,[36] as commissioner of works in charge of government hospitality, thanked Lord Derby for his help in the task of arranging entertainment for overseas visitors.[37] Again, in 1935, Wilson Taylor told Lord Derby, 'the Foreign Office want us to give the dinner to all the members of the Naval Conference of all Nations' (26 November 1935). As Wilson Taylor pointed out to the American Pilgrims in 1930: 'At the present time we maintain our standard as the premier dining club in London: and by being non-political – yet helpful to the Government in power of whatever party – we attain a certain semi-official status also.'

Notable events in the 1930s included a dinner on 16 May 1933 in honour of the Prime Minister, J. Ramsay MacDonald, and a celebration on 30 April 1935 of King George V's Silver Jubilee. The guest of honour at the Silver Jubilee banquet was the Duke of Kent, newly elected an honorary member of the Pilgrims, and other speakers included the American ambassador, Robert Bingham, the Governor-General of Canada, John Buchan, and the Lord Chief Justice, Lord Hewart. There was a dinner on 12 July 1932 to celebrate the bicentenary of the birth of George

J. Ramsay MacDonald

Washington: this was one of several events organised by the bicentenary committee at the United States embassy. J. Wilson Taylor represented the Pilgrims on this committee, which decided there would be a Pilgrims dinner, a reception at the American embassy, a gathering at Sulgrave Manor, and a dinner hosted by various other Anglo-American societies in London, including the American Society and the American Club. One of the speakers at this dinner was Winston Churchill, MP, who declared that whatever problems faced the two nations, 'I believe that there is one grand valiant conviction shared on both sides of the Atlantic. It is this: together, there is no problem we cannot solve.' The dinners for the ambassadors

were as popular as ever: for the welcome dinner for Andrew Mellon on 14 April 1932, when the Prince of Wales spoke, there were 400 guests – 34 round tables, and a chairman's table of 52 – and a long waiting list of those who applied too late. The Pilgrims continued to entertain visiting sportsmen, feeling that this had an important contribution to make to future Anglo-American relations[38]. The last dinner for a distinguished statesman from the Dominions was in 1931, the dinner

Andrew Mellon

for the Earl of Willingdon, Viceroy-designate of India, who was retiring as Governor-General of Canada. After this, the Pilgrims functions became wholly Anglo-American, unlike in the early days, when, perhaps because of Harry Brittain's interest in the Empire, there were a number of such events.

The dinner to celebrate the coronation of King George VI was the only big function in 1937, but early in 1938 Joseph Kennedy arrived in London as the new American ambassador. Ambassador Kennedy, as he insisted on calling himself for the rest of his life, was the first Irish-American and the first Catholic to be appointed to the Court of St James, and was warmly welcomed by the Pilgrims. He worked hard on his speech, sending drafts both to President Roosevelt and the Secretary of State, Cordell Hull, intending it to be an important statement of American foreign policy. Although he emphasised the desire of most Americans to stay out of a European war, the speech was well received:[39]

> 'My country has decided that it must stand on its own feet . . . The United States has no intention of attacking anyone. It does not expect to be attacked. It is now, and intends to remain, on friendly terms with every country in the world. If the force of events should make it impossible for us to follow this policy, my country will decide, when the time comes, what to do to preserve the welfare of its own citizens.'

Kennedy's attitude reflected the mood of many Americans in the 1930s, and the memory of how the United States had failed to stay out of the First World War. But by the time he was recalled to Washington he was very unpopular in London, not only among the British, but among Americans as well, because of his reports during the Blitz that Britain was doomed, and that America must not intervene to save her. The Pilgrims were spared the embarrassment of deciding

Joseph Kennedy

whether to give him a farewell dinner, because he returned to America for good in December 1940, several months before his resignation was announced.

Winston Churchill, Prime Minister since Neville Chamberlain's resignation on 10 May 1940, attended his first Pilgrims function since 1932 when he spoke at the din-

ner on 9 January 1941 in honour of Lord Halifax, ambassador-designate to Washington, who was to replace Lord Lothian, who had died in America. He began his speech by saying:

'The future of the whole world and the hopes of a broadening civilisation founded upon Christian ethics depend upon the relations between the British Empire . . . and of the United States of America. The identity of purpose and persistence of

Winston Churchill

resolve prevailing throughout the English-speaking world will more than any other single fact determine the way of life that will be open to the generations, and perhaps to the centuries, which follow our own . . . We stand therefore – all of us – upon the watchtowers of history.'

Two months later, 455 Pilgrims and their guests, including the Prime Minister and most members of the Cabinet, welcomed John Winant as the new American ambassador to Britain. His devotion to the British cause was especially welcome after the ambassadorship of the unpopular and defeatist Kennedy. Described by one observer as a more human version of Abraham Lincoln, Winant was to make a great impact in Britain. At the lunch on 18 March 1941, Churchill told Winant:

'We welcome you to this Island at a moment when a great battle in which your Government and nation are deeply interested is developing its full scope and severity. The battle of the Atlantic must be won in a decisive manner; it must be won beyond all doubt if the declared policies of the Government and the people of the United States are not to be forcibly frustrated . . . Mr Winant, you come to us at a grand turning point in the world's history.'

In his reply, Winant told his audience:

'Today it is the honour and destiny of the British people to man the bridgehead of humanity's hopes. It is their privilege to stand against ruthless and powerful dictators who would destroy the lessons of two thousand years of history. It is your destiny to say to them, "Here you shall not pass."'

These important speeches were recorded, broadcast that evening to the British public, and relayed to North America. During the lunch at the Savoy, ack-ack guns began firing on the Embankment, and this led Winant to tell his neighbour that he had that morning come across a woman in Islington in the ruins of her home, arranging a few sprigs of lilac in a broken vase, which she filled from a fireman's hose, and that he knew then why the Nazis could never win: 'What chance has Hitler got against her?' Lord Derby, although in poor health, and partly crippled after a car accident the previous year, presided at both lunches.[40] Meanwhile, messages of support arrived from the American Pilgrims. Elihu Church, the secretary, wrote to Wilson Taylor: 'Words are inadequate to give any idea of our admiration of the fighting spirit of the people of Britain and the Commonwealth . . . You are the bulwark of civilization. I would to God . . . that we were in the fight with you, and in a position to be of real assistance. I think we will be in before long' (28 June 1940). In November, the American Pilgrims paid for two mobile canteen trailers, as a token of their admiration for the courage of the British people during the air raids. On 8 December 1941, after the attack on Pearl Harbor, the United States declared war on Japan, and three days later Germany declared war on the United States. Although there was some discussion about organising a club for American officers in London, as in 1917, and a subcommittee of the Pilgrims was set up, Sir John Wilson Taylor and Lord Derby decided to let someone else do it this time, and the idea was not pursued.[41] There was only one other Pilgrims function during the war, a lunch in 1943 for Lord Wavell, the new Viceroy of India. When it was suggested that the Pilgrims might entertain Alexander Woollcott, the

American humorist, Wilson Taylor wrote that the committee had decided to restrict hospitality to 'distinguished personages associated with war activities'.[42]

Lord Derby became president of the Pilgrims in 1945, succeeding the Duke of Connaught, who had died in 1942.[43] The new chairman, Hamar Greenwood, 1st Viscount Greenwood, a Canadian, presided at his first function, a dinner to welcome the Prime Minister, Clement Attlee, back from a visit to North America, on 5 December 1945. This was the first of several import-ant postwar dinners, including one for Eleanor Roosevelt, widow of President Roosevelt. She was the first woman to be guest of honour at a Pilgrims func-

Viscount Greenwood

tion. The Pilgrims were so busy in 1946 that John Winant, the retiring American ambassador, and Lord Inverchapel, the new British ambassador to Washington, had to share a dinner, as did Lord Halifax, newly returned from Washington, and Averell Harriman, the new American ambassador. At the dinner for John Winant, after Lord Greenwood had suggested that Winant was the greatest American ambassador there had ever been, Anthony Eden, the former Foreign Secretary, and a close friend, supported the toast:

Eleanor Roosevelt

'I must try . . . to tell you why we honour Mr Winant. First, because as ambassador he was and is truly representative of his great country, and never forgot it. Secondly, because he believed in our cause and in our will and ability to defend that cause, in the hour when we stood alone.
Thirdly, because no fairer, straighter man has ever walked this earth.'

Perhaps the most important postwar dinner was that on 12 December 1947 at the Dorchester Hotel, for George Marshall, the Secretary of State of the United States. Marshall had first proposed American financial aid for a programme of European economic recovery in a famous speech at Harvard in June 1947, and the Marshall Plan for Europe was implemented in 1948. In his speech to the Pilgrims, his only speech in England, Marshall distinguished between a "special

George Marshall

relationship" and a "natural relationship", regarding the relationship between Britain and the United States as the latter: 'There is no more natural relationship in international life than that between the United States and the British Commonwealth. This relationship requires no special political initiative. It is not embodied in any formal treaty or pact.'

These dinners, and those of the 1950s, led Lord Halifax, president of the Pilgrims from 1950 to 1958, to state in his memoirs, *Fulness of Days* (1957), that the main activity of the Society was to entertain and provide a platform for distinguished Americans when they visited Britain, but to the outside world the most important thing the Pilgrims did in these years was to initiate and take charge of the erecting of the Franklin Roosevelt Memorial in Grosvenor Square.

It was Sir Campbell Stuart, a member of the Pilgrims executive committee since 1919, who suggested the idea to Lord Derby. Sir Campbell was experienced in the matter of setting up statues: he had chaired a committee of the Canadian History Society which erected a statue of General Wolfe at Greenwich in 1930, and also sat on the Mansion House committee which raised money for a memorial to King George V, taking over the chairmanship from Attlee in 1945.[44] The scheme was launched at the dinner for Eleanor Roosevelt in February 1946, when a letter from Lord Derby was read out. Ever since President Roosevelt's death in April 1945, suggestions for a memorial had been pouring into the government and had been aired in the press, including a proposal to name the new airport at Staines (the present Heathrow Airport) "Port Roosevelt", as thousands of Americans would make their first landing in England there. The two main alternatives appeared to be a hospital specialising in infantile paralysis (polio) and a statue, and although at first the government intended to take charge of the project, which would be paid for out of public funds, in the end they decided to let the Pilgrims go ahead and do all the organisation themselves. The Pilgrims set up a committee, chaired by Lord Greenwood, and soon settled on a statue, to be placed in Grosvenor

Sir Campbell Stuart

Square, because of its long associations with the United States: John Adams, the first American minister to Britain, from 1786 to 1788, and later second President of the United States, lived there, as did Walter Hines Page, the American ambassador at the time of the First World War. During the Second World War John Winant lived in a flat in the embassy, and it was the centre for the American armed forces. The Duke of Westminster, who owned the land, agreed to give it to the nation, and the Prime Minister steered a special Act of Parliament

Lord Halifax

through the House of Commons, because of the law safeguarding open spaces in London, while the residents gave up their exclusive rights to the use of the garden. Introducing the bill, in October 1946, the Prime Minister said of Roosevelt:

'Here, in this House today, we think of him mainly as a great upholder of freedom and democracy, and as the loyal and true friend of this country. No one saw more clearly than did he that our fight against Hitlerism was a fight for freedom all over the world, and he recognised that in the dark days of 1940, Britain was holding the outpost line of liberty before that realisation had come to many of his countrymen.'

Supporting the bill, Winston Churchill said:

'Of Roosevelt, however, it must be said that had he not acted when he did, in the way he did, had he not felt the generous surge of freedom in his heart, had he not resolved to give aid to Britain and Europe in the supreme crisis through which we have passed, a hideous fate might well have overwhelmed mankind and made its whole future for centuries sink into shame and ruin. It may well be that the man whom we honour today not only anticipated history but altered its course, and altered it in a manner which has saved the freedom and earned the gratitude of the human race for generations to come.'

The committee asked Sir William Reid Dick, RA, to make the statue: it was he who had made the statue of George V, and his statue of David Livingstone at Victoria Falls was also well known. After much controversy over whether it should be a sitting or standing statue, John Winant was consulted, and he felt that Mrs Roosevelt would prefer a standing statue. The committee decided that as the memorial was to be a tribute from the British people, as many British people as possible should be given the opportunity to contribute, and all offers from American sources were refused. The cost was estimated to be £40,000, and the public was invited to contribute to a maximum of five shillings per person. The appeal was launched by the Prime Minister on the BBC on 17 November 1946. Special booths were set up in London, where people could make their contributions, and the rest of the population was invited to post theirs in. That the target was reached in five days demonstrated the high regard that the people of Britain had for the late President.

On 12 April 1948, three years after the death of Roosevelt, on a glorious sunny day, Eleanor Roosevelt unveiled the statue in the presence of the King and Queen, other members of the Royal Family, members of the government and armed forces, and Pilgrims. The Royal Marines lined the route, and the service was conducted by Geoffrey Fisher, Archbishop of Canterbury and a vice-president of the Pilgrims. That evening Eleanor Roosevelt was guest of honour at what was perhaps the greatest dinner in the history of the Pilgrims. Over nine hundred guests including Princess Elizabeth and the Duke of Edinburgh, in their first public appearance since their wedding in November 1947, took over the whole ground floor of the Savoy Hotel, and it was the first occasion to which members' wives and daughters were invited as guests. Thanks to weeks of detailed planning on the part of Sir Campbell Stuart and Hugh Wontner, general manager of the Savoy, everything went smoothly, and nine hundred hot dinners were served to the guests, while the rest of the hotel guests were undisturbed.[45]

Sir Campbell Stuart was chairman from 1948 to 1958. He had been a member of the executive committee since 1919, and after his retirement as chairman remained chairman of the dinner committee until 1968.[46] Sir Campbell was in many ways like Harry Brittain. He knew everybody, he loved organising, he paid great attention to detail, and he used his connections in the newspaper world[47] to ensure maximum publicity for the Pilgrims. He also maintained a weekly exchange of letters with Gano Dunn, chairman of the American Pilgrims until 1953, by means of which they kept each other abreast of Pilgrims affairs and in touch with who was likely to be crossing the Atlantic, just as Harry Brittain had corresponded with George Wilson in New York.[48] And like Harry Brittain, he did not allow the world to forget the pre-eminent position of the Pilgrims.[49] During most of Stuart's chairmanship, the president was Lord Halifax, former Foreign Secretary, and British ambassador in Washington from 1941 to 1946.[50] The partnership was very successful: Lord Halifax was a respected elder statesman, who lent distinction to Pilgrims functions, but like Lord Derby, he preferred to spend most of his time in the country, at Garrowby, the family seat in Yorkshire.[51]

After the war, and particularly after all the publicity surrounding the unveiling of the Roosevelt statue, there were a number of people who wanted to join the Pilgrims. In 1946 the membership was limited to six hundred, and the waiting list grew.[52] But by the end of 1956 there were already 651 members, and a waiting list of 150. Although there was nothing in the rules of the society to say that candidates must have some American association, the membership committee tried to take this into consideration.

During the ten years of his chairmanship, Sir Campbell Stuart lured some glittering names to the Pilgrims dinners, even making special trips to America to do so, as when he tried, and failed, to persuade the American Secretary of State, John Foster Dulles, to come in 1958, personally conveying the invitation to Washington.[53] There were rarely more than two functions a year, and sometimes only one, and although the Pilgrims continued to hold the traditional dinners for the new American ambassadors to Britain, none of the British ambassadors-designate to Washington managed a dinner.[54] Other notable occasions included a dinner for Dean Acheson, American Secretary of State, in 1950, at which Acheson noted that : 'A strange and confusing dissonance has crowded the trans-Atlantic frequencies . . . The dissonance flows from the very awareness that difficult decisions must be made and is a part of the process of making them.'

The Pilgrims entertained Anthony Eden, the Foreign Secretary, in 1952, Harry Truman, ex-President of the United States, in 1956, and Vice-President Richard Nixon in November 1958, shortly after Sir Campbell Stuart's retirement. After the deterioration in relations between Britain and the United States over the Suez crisis of November 1956, it was at a Pilgrims dinner that John Hay Whitney, the new American ambassador, was able to report on the positive outcome of the

John Hay Whitney

Bermuda conference between Prime Minister Harold Macmillan and President Eisenhower and their secretaries of state.

'I would like to say something more of the spirit underlying the Bermuda conference. In our meeting was the proof that a true and strong friendship can stand up to adversity.

'The quality of an alliance is assured by the ability to survive internal differences. Through such differences in our diplomatic consciences we faced that trial at Suez. Our paths diverged. Suspicion ran between us, and confusion, and lack of understanding. But if we parted company at Suez, the Bermuda conference marked the point of our return.'[55]

Geoffrey Fisher,
Archbishop of Canterbury

Many people felt that the highlight of these years was the speech delivered by Geoffrey Fisher, Archbishop of Canterbury, at the dinner in his honour on 16 November 1954. So many people wrote asking for copies of the speech after hearing it broadcast on the BBC that the Pilgrims printed extra copies, although they usually only sent copies to members.[56] The archbishop concluded his speech with the following passage:

'So we find the true secret of Anglo-American relationship and friendship. They cannot become like us; their history and their setting is quite different. We could, if we wished, try to imitate them, blowing ourselves out to compete with them, lengthening the small steps of the tubby figure of John Bull in order to keep pace with the long strides of Uncle Sam. But we should be wrong. Our work in the world and for the world can only be done by our proportions, as America must do her work with her proportions. But we need each other greatly for the health of us both, and the world for its preservation desperately needs what our wholehearted trust and co-operation can bring to it. We need America to keep us moving, eager and young for our years and still adventurous. America needs us to keep her patient, sensitive, and aware that if size often shows on a great scale the splendours of God, His deepest secrets are to be found only in the small, simple and domestic.'

In the 1950s there seemed to be a cooling-off of relations between the Pilgrims and the BBC. While Sir Campbell Stuart was well aware of the importance of broadcasting,[57] and wanted the BBC to continue to broadcast speeches at Pilgrims dinners, he resisted the idea that events should be televised, especially as the BBC did not want to cover the whole event, but just the most important speeches. One of the biggest clashes was over the dinner for Eden on 18 June 1952: the BBC wanted to televise half an hour of the event, starting at 9.30, covering Eden's speech, but Stuart wanted it to start at nine, and last an hour, to take in his own opening speech, and those of Jowitt and Halifax. He tried to persuade George Barnes, Director of Television, that the public would like to see the pageantry of a Pilgrims dinner: 'The Pilgrims dinner that night with twenty Ambassadors and leading citizens of the land all in full evening dress with decorations would make a brilliant picture.'[58] But when the BBC would not budge, because the total television transmission each evening was only two hours, and more than half an hour would take too great a portion of it, Stuart said they would have to dispense with television altogether. However, Sir Campbell had a change of mind the following year and tried very hard to persuade the BBC to televise the Pilgrims' 50th anniversary dinner. In a letter to Seymour de Lotbiniere, Director of Outside Broadcasts, he painted a colourful picture of toasts with special fanfares by sixteen trumpeters from the Royal Military School of Music, but this time it was the BBC who turned down the idea.[59] Many Pilgrims thought the glare of the television lights would be distracting, so he even went to the lengths of organising a lighting test in an empty banqueting room before deciding whether to allow television cameras in to the farewell dinner for Ambassador Winthrop Aldrich in 1957.[60] In the end, Pilgrims events were not televised, and there was also a decline in interest on the part of the BBC in broadcasting Pilgrims dinners at all. The last live broadcast was from the farewell dinner for Ambassador Bruce in 1961, although on a few subsequent occasions speeches were recorded for later transmission in Britain and overseas.

The last function that Sir Campbell Stuart organised as chairman was the lunch for Vice-President Nixon on 25 November 1958, although he had retired by then and was

Vice-President Nixon

not there himself. He had been trying for some time to get Nixon to a Pilgrims dinner: in 1953 when he thought Nixon was coming to England, and in 1957 when he was expected to come to the meeting of the American Bar Association in London. This was Nixon's first visit to England, and his first official function there. Stuart worked hard to make the lunch a success, and was particularly anxious to discuss Nixon's speech with him in advance, but despite a trip to the United States beforehand he was unable to see him. He invited

Lord Birkett

leading members of the press, including Lord Rothermere (owner of the *Daily Sketch*), Cecil King (chairman of the *Daily Mirror)*, and Laurence Scott (chairman of the *Manchester Guardian)*, and among the Pilgrims present were Lord Astor of Hever (owner of *The Times*), Viscount Astor, and Lord Iliffe (owner of the *Birmingham Post*). In a letter to Lord Birkett, the new president, before the committee dinner on 23 October 1958 to mark Sir Campbell Stuart's retirement, Tony Gishford, the Pilgrims secretary, wrote that 'Apart from *The Times*, The Pilgrims has been the real love of his life.'[61] In his tribute to Sir Campbell Stuart at the dinner, Lord Birkett said: 'He has brought The Pilgrims to a pinnacle of excellence. I do not see how the prestige of The Pilgrims could stand higher than it stands today. In its field, and in what it sets out to do, the light of this great Anglo-American society shines forth.'

For the next ten years no one person was really in charge of running the Pilgrims. The chairman was Sir Christopher Chancellor,[62] general manager of Reuters, continuing the tradition of appointing a chairman with strong links to

the press. Tony Gishford continued as honorary secretary until 1964. Lord Halifax had resigned the presidency at the same time as Sir Campbell Stuart gave up the chairmanship, and was succeeded by two distinguished lawyers, Lord Birkett from 1958 to 1962, and Lord Evershed[63] from 1962 to 1965. Lord Harlech (formerly David Ormsby Gore) became president in 1965, beginning a twelve-year stint. There were sometimes long gaps between functions: there was only one in

Sir Christopher Chancellor 1959 and 1960, and nothing between August 1962

and December 1963, or between March 1966 and June 1967. Lord Birkett presided at every function held during his presidency, and Lord Evershed presided at three of the five dinners held during his tenure of office. Sir Campbell Stuart continued to exert his influence through his chairmanship of the dinner committee, and through his friend, Tony Gishford,[64] especially after Gishford's stroke in 1962, when Sir Campbell looked after things while Gishford was ill and Sir Christopher Chancellor was too busy. During

Lord Evershed

these years the Pilgrims gave a welcome dinner for the only new American ambassador, David Bruce, in 1961, and send-offs for the British ambassadors-designate David Ormsby Gore in 1961 and Sir Patrick Dean[65] in 1965. The speeches at the farewell dinner on 11 January 1961 for Ambassador John Hay Whitney made a big impact, with a long report in *The Times*. Whitney emphasised the need for Britain and the United States to explain themselves more candidly to each other:

> 'Within the past two weeks on the basis of a totally false rumour that the United States wanted to use force in Laos, an extraordinary picture of a trigger-happy America has been circulated here among you, our British friends. It is the picture of an irresponsible Power being held back with difficulty from the brink of war by its Allies. I simply cannot believe that this is really what you think of us, or of the President who has worked with such devotion for eight years in the cause of peace. Yet I am disturbed, and most, I think, by the fact that this caricature of the United States sprang apparently so spontaneously to mind in a situation where admittedly there was scant access to facts . . .
>
>   'Anti-Americanism, like its ugly sister, Anglophobia, I am convinced does not spring from the heart. I am perfectly sure that neither has anything to do with the brain. In fact, I do not worry about malice in itself. What troubles me is that by inattention to things malice feeds on we may let ourselves become entangled in quarrels we did not intend and which have no substance and no rational cause.'

The most popular function was the lunch for ex-President Eisenhower on 14 August 1962: there were 450 Pilgrims and guests, including many of Eisenhower's wartime colleagues,[66] and a long waiting list. At this lunch the Pilgrims also celebrated their Diamond Jubilee, and Lord Evershed read out a message of congratulations from the Queen, Patron of the Pilgrims: 'It is a fine tribute to their work in the cause of Anglo-American friendship over sixty years to have General Eisenhower as their honoured guest at luncheon.' General Eisenhower made a plea for greater mutual understanding:

Dwight D. Eisenhower

'Knowledge and understanding cannot guarantee peace, but . . . without mutual understanding there will never be peace . . . Between ourselves, we must do better what we have done up to now. Between us, the progress toward understanding that has been made by such organizations as The Pilgrims must continue: we must rededicate ourselves to the problem of creating mutual understanding – everywhere in the world.'

Other functions included a dinner for George Woods, president of the World Bank, on 29 November 1965, to which a number of leading bankers were invited, and a dinner for John McCloy, chairman of the Ford Foundation.[67] There were some disappointments: they tried and failed to get President Kennedy to agree to a dinner in his honour when he visited Britain in June 1961 – no serving American President has ever been to a Pilgrims dinner – and a lunch for U Thant, secretary-general of the United Nations, organised for May 1967, had to be cancelled at the last minute.

The Foreign Office continued to keep a close eye on what went on at Pilgrims dinners, regarding these as a good opportunity to make foreign policy statements. When the government was embarrassed by the hostile American reaction to the enthusiastic welcome given by the British public in 1961 to the Russian astronaut Yuri Gagarin, the first man in space, a memo was sent to Edward Heath, Lord Privy Seal, suggesting that he should get some mild corrective into his Pilgrims speech that evening: 'The Pilgrims tonight provide an ideal occasion, with a captive American audience.'[68] When his private office was preparing the speech that the Foreign Secretary, Michael Stewart, was to make to the Pilgrims on 29 March

1965, the American department of the Foreign Office was asked for some notes: 'I would be grateful for some notes on the stock-in-trade of Pilgrim speeches – Anglo-American relations, avoiding if possible some of the more trans-Atlantic clichés.'[69]

Lord Astor

Another important period in the history of the Pilgrims began in 1967 with the appointment of Gavin Astor[70] as the new chairman: he remained chairman until 1977, and then president until 1983. He became chairman at a time when a lot of people were losing interest in the Pilgrims. There were fewer applications for membership, which was still restricted to men, while a number of previously male societies were opening their doors to women (even the American Pilgrims had been inviting ladies – though not admitting them as members – since the early 1950s). The only women invited to Pilgrims events were invited *ex officio*,[71] and there was a growing feeling that the Pilgrims were old fashioned and out of touch. Astor and the committee were worried that so many eminent men were refusing invitations to dinners:

Lord Harlech

Senator Fulbright, Senator Robert Kennedy, Robert Macnamara, and Dean Rusk all refused, as did the Duke of Edinburgh. Gavin Astor was 49 when he became chairman, and Lord Harlech, president since 1965, was the same age. Not since the days of Harry Brittain had the Pilgrims been in the hands of such young men (Harry Brittain, of course, was a lot younger), and Astor was keen to make changes. In January 1968 he drafted a long document, which he sent to all members of the executive committee, including the following lines:

'The object of the Society is to promote Anglo-American good-fellowship. The rules do not specify that this shall be done merely at formal luncheons or dinners. But over the years it seems that the Pilgrims Society has come to be recognised primarily as a very distinguished Dining Club. There is a danger here that excessive delusions of grandeur may cause the Society to assume a sense of importance to which in fact it has no claim.

'The present function of individual Pilgrims is reduced to eating occasional dinners and listening to speeches by other people. Many Pilgrims would like personally to contribute more to the Society and to the fulfilment of its object.

'If the Pilgrims Society is to continue simply as an exclusive dining club, then its influence is likely to lose its point.' [72]

After several meetings to discuss this, and correspondence with Sir Paul Gore-Booth, head of the Foreign Office,[73] Astor outlined his plans for revitalising the society at the Annual Meeting on 17 July 1968. His main worry was that the Pilgrims should be more than just an exclusive dining club, and he made a number of suggestions. He wanted to copy the American Pilgrims and have more frequent and less formal functions, including an evening reception to which ladies could be invited, and informal lunches, as well as three or four big dinners a year. He and his wife had already invited the Pilgrims and their ladies to an afternoon party at Hever Castle in October 1967, which had been a great success,[74] and this was followed by the first Pilgrims reception, on 4 December 1969, at the Middle Temple Hall. Ladies were invited to a dinner on 4 October 1971 for members of the American embassy and their wives, and to a "Dining In" night at the Savoy on 30 November 1972, but they were not invited to a proper formal dinner, with speeches, until 1974, the farewell dinner for Ambassador Walter Annenberg – and this was because Mrs Annenberg insisted.[75] Astor was also very anxious to extend membership to younger people: he pointed out that the average age of the membership committee was 74. As a gesture in this direction he invited his son to the "Dining In" night on 30 November 1972, and encouraged other members to do the same, so that at one table there were eleven young people.[76] The Pilgrims had increased the membership limit to 750, but in 1970 they were still about seventy short of the maximum. One problem was that Sir Harry Brittain, chairman of the membership committee, did not like the idea of electing those on the existing waiting list. He was supported in this by Sir Campbell Stuart, who felt that a club without a waiting list was not worth joining, and that to be elected a Pilgrim always used to be considered a privilege. He also pointed out that the American Pilgrims, with a larger membership, had a ten-year waiting list, as did a number of London clubs, including Pratt's Club, and White's, which had an even longer one.[77] In 1972 the numbers were still comparatively low, with only 659 paying members, and no waiting list.[78]

Astor was greatly helped by the new honorary secretary, Lt-Col Stuart Chant-Sempill, appointed in 1968. Chant-Sempill made a number of suggestions, especially as to who to invite to dinners.[79] It was he who suggested inviting Ronald Reagan, tipped as the number-one contender for the Republican nomination in the next presidential election. The Pilgrims were already planning to entertain Senator Henry "Scoop" Jackson, the leading Democratic contender (who had asked to be invited), at a dinner on 11 November 1974.

Ronald Reagan

Chant-Sempill organised the Reagan dinner through General Gruenther, with whom

Lt-Col Stuart Chant-Sempill

he had served after the war, as he was accompanying Reagan on his trip to England. In April 1974 General Gruenther told Chant-Sempill that Reagan would like to be invited to a Pilgrims dinner: 'there is a sudden realisation in the States as to the importance of the Pilgrims over here. It is indeed a signal honour and completely justifies what we decided in your house earlier this year – to invite more important American speakers to our functions'.[80] It was also Chant-Sempill's idea to have a banquet in the Mansion House while Sir Hugh Wontner, chairman of the Savoy Hotel Group, was Lord Mayor, as a special tribute to Sir Hugh and in recognition of the long connection of the Pilgrims with the Savoy Hotel. Chant-Sempill remained as secretary until his death in 1991.

Despite Astor's ambition to increase the number of functions, the Pilgrims soon settled down to three or four events a year, including one annual reception (except 1970, 1975 and 1977) at places such as the Middle Temple, Winfield House, the House of Lords and the Banqueting House in Whitehall. Although he had proposed six informal lunches a year, there were only a few, including lunches for the Chancellor of the Exchequer, Roy Jenkins,[81] on 24 October 1968, and the American composer Leonard Bernstein,[82] on 25 February 1970. The

Sir Hugh Wontner

Lord Cromer

tradition that the new American ambassador should make his first public speech in England to the Pilgrims continued,[83] with welcome dinners for Walter Annenberg[84] on 28 May 1969, Elliott Richardson on 11 March 1975, and Anne Armstrong on 31 March 1976, and there were dinners for British ambassadors, including that for the Earl of Cromer on 11 January 1971. The Pilgrims continued to entertain British politicians, including the former Prime Minister Edward Heath, on 9 February 1976,[85] and distinguished American guests included General Alexander Haig, Supreme Allied Commander Europe, on 20 October 1975. Prince Charles was the guest of honour on 8 December 1970, renewing the tradition of the inter-war years, when the Prince of Wales was a frequent guest at Pilgrims functions. One of the biggest coups was to get the American Secretary of State, Henry Kissinger,[86] to a dinner on 12 December 1973. Originally planned for October, it had had to be postponed because of the Middle East situation, and the occasion was seen in Washington as a valuable opportunity to discuss the strains in the alliance caused by the Middle East crisis. In a long and important speech, which was given wide press coverage, including a front-page report in *The Times*,

Prince Charles

Kissinger called for a renewal of the Atlantic community, and warned that European unity must not be allowed to damage the North Atlantic alliance. He concluded by saying:

Henry Kissinger

'We have every reason of duty and self-interest to preserve the most successful partnership in history. The United States is committed to making the Atlantic Community a vital positive force for the future as it was for the past. What has recently been taken for granted must now be renewed. This is not an American challenge to Europe; it is history's challenge to us all.'

The Pilgrims felt that this dinner 'put the Pilgrims back into the limelight'.[87]

On 25 January 1972, the Pilgrims celebrated their 70th anniversary with a dinner at the Savoy. Sir Harry Brittain,[88] recently elected "Pilgrim Emeritus", was the guest of honour, and blew out the candles on the birthday cake, presented with the compliments of the Savoy. The Speaker of the House of Commons, Selwyn Lloyd, proposed the toast: he was asked to do this because the Pilgrims had always attached great importance to their association with the House of Commons, and this was traditionally symbolised by the Speaker becoming one of the vice-presidents. The anniversary year continued with a reception at St James's Palace, attended by the Queen Mother (and one of her corgis), on 5 July, and a reception at the Royal Academy with a private view of the Armand Hammer Collection of Old Masters and Impressionist paintings.

The biggest event of these years was the Bicentennial Dinner on 6 July 1976, one of the hottest days of the hot summer of 1976. This was before the days of air-conditioning at the Savoy, and the fans were filled with ice in an attempt to cool the room, filled to capacity (the stage had been removed to make room for more guests).[89] The Queen Mother was the guest of honour,[90] making her first-ever after-dinner speech. After recalling her official visit to America in 1939, when she and the King stayed with the Roosevelts, she said:

> 'The Americans . . . have shared with us many years of recorded history. Their laws are based on the English Common Law. The language of the Declaration of Independence was the language of Shakespeare. And they have, in reply, Longfellow and Henry James; and it has been continually enriched by contributions from both sides of the Atlantic.
>
> 'These ties of culture, after some initial difficulties not unknown, endured through thick and thin until finally cemented by our shared responsibility in two world wars, in the second of which we worked together as closely as two allies have ever worked together in the past.'

As part of their contribution to the bicentennial celebrations in England, the Pilgrims were the moving spirit behind an exhibition at the Victoria and Albert Museum, "American Art: 1750–1800. Towards Independence", organised by the V&A in conjunction with the Pilgrims, the Arts Council and Yale University. Tony Gishford first approached Sir John Pope-Hennessy, director of the V&A (and a Pilgrim), with the idea in 1970, and was closely involved in the planning, and responsible for raising

Robert Sigmon

funds for the exhibition. Lord Harlech, president of the Pilgrims, was chairman of the exhibition committee. After Tony Gishford's death in 1975, his place was taken by Robert Sigmon, a member of the Pilgrims executive committee, and future chairman. Over two hundred works were exhibited, including paintings, furniture, silver and gold, pewter, ceramics, glass and textiles, showing the excellence and variety of artistic production in America during the years of transition from the late colonial period to that of independence, and it was the first time that the British public had had the opportunity to see a major exhibition of early American art. [91]

On 18 July 1977 the Pilgrims agreed in principle to admit women members. As long ago as 1955, the committee had discussed the proposal put forward by Professor George Catlin[92] that women be eligible for membership, but the decision that the suggestion was unacceptable was unanimous (even though there was nothing in the rules limiting the membership to men). By 1974, the committee had received a number of letters raising the issue, and again it was discussed and rejected, although it was agreed to renew the discussion from time to time, and to continue to invite women as guests to selected Pilgrims functions. The decision taken by the Pilgrims of the United States in April 1977 to elect women[93] forced their hand, as according to the constitution anyone elected a member in one country automatically became a member of the sister society. The proposal was received by the English committee 'in silent acquiescence rather than spontaneous enthusiasm',[94] and no women were put forward for election until 1978, when Baroness Elliot of Harwood became a Pilgrim.[95]

Lord Astor remained concerned about the future of the Pilgrims, and before he retired as president in 1983 he wrote to Robert Sigmon, the chairman, setting out his thoughts.[96] His main concern was that the Society was still living on its past reputation, and that only a very small number of the membership attended any functions, so that most members had no idea what was going on in the Society. He speculated on the possible reasons for this poor attendance:

Baroness Elliot of Harwood

'One wonders in fact why so few of our members attend the dinners? Are they too expensive? Are they too formal? Should a period of Questions and Answers be permitted after the formal speeches? Do some of them regard it as a not worthwhile evening out in both time and expense to find themselves sitting next to some stranger – male or female – with nothing in common, particularly if they are not members of the Society. Should there be more social evenings and receptions in unusual and interesting venues?'

Lord Astor called for a reappraisal of the objects and public image of the Pilgrims, and of its value to its members.[97]

Robert Sigmon, a lawyer, and the first American to be chairman of the British Pilgrims, took over following the Annual Meeting at Hever Castle on 18 July 1977, which was also a celebration of the diamond jubilee of the Society. Recommended by Lord Sherfield as 'by far the most active and dedicated member of the Executive Committee',[98] he agreed to be chairman on the understanding that if the president were unable to preside at a function one of the vice-presidents would: he was prepared to do the administrative work of chairman, but he did not want to take on the social side.[99] He was joined by Lord Carrington, the new president, in 1983, when Lord Astor retired. Sigmon continued the pattern of events laid down by Astor, with occasional lunches, one or two formal dinners a year (usually at the Savoy, although in the late 1980s several dinners were held at Claridge's[100]), and an increasing number of informal receptions at interesting venues, including Lambeth Palace in 1978, St James's Palace in 1979 (in honour of the Queen and Prince Philip), the House of Lords in 1987, and the Bank of England in 1991. Some of these began with a speaker and a question-and-answer session: the first was in 1981, a very successful

Lord Carrington

event, when Eugene Rostow, director of the US Arms Control and Disarmament Agency, spoke at a reception at the American embassy. The Pilgrims continued to give dinners to welcome the new American ambassadors: Kingman Brewster in 1977, John Louis in 1981, Charles Price in 1984, Henry Catto in 1989, and Raymond Seitz in 1991. The tradition of giving dinners for British ambassadors to Washington on their departure and return waned a little, with only two farewell dinners, for Sir Anthony Acland in 1986 and Sir Robin Renwick in 1991, although there were several

Sir Anthony Acland

receptions for them, including a farewell party for Sir Nicholas Henderson in 1979 and a party to welcome Sir Oliver Wright back in 1986. The Pilgrims gave a series of dinners for important British and American political figures, including three British Foreign Secretaries: David Owen on 13 March 1978, Geoffrey Howe on 13 February 1986, and Douglas Hurd on 18 July 1990. There was a lunch for George Schultz, Secretary of State of the United States, on 10 December 1985, and Caspar Weinberger, Secretary of Defense of the United States, was guest of honour at a dinner on 21 June 1983. Henry Kissinger became one of very few distinguished people on either side of the Atlantic (other than ambassadors) to have a second dinner in his honour, when he was entertained at the Savoy on 21 January 1988. The most important Pilgrims dinner during this period was the dinner for the Prime Minister, Mrs Margaret Thatcher, on 29 January 1981. Ignoring the fact that the Pilgrims had always regarded themselves as non-political, she made a highly political speech, comparing the policies of her own government with those of Ronald Reagan, the new President of the United States. Turning to foreign policy, she discussed the effect of Britain's membership of the European Community on the Atlantic alliance:

Sir Nicholas Henderson

'Now I am often asked, will Britain's membership of the Economic Community change things. I believe that it can't and won't lessen the friendship between the United States and Britain . . . In linking herself with the European Community, Britain has joined a group of nations which themselves have close family ties across the Atlantic.

'And nor does closer co-operation within the European Community between the countries itself threaten those links. Because a stronger, more self-confident Europe, pursuing more cohesive policies will produce a greater area of stability for democracy . . .

'The Atlantic partnership is and will remain by far the most important bulwark in the worldwide defence of liberty and democracy.'

Inevitably, there were some disappointments. The Pilgrims had hoped to entertain the Prince and Princess of Wales in 1983 to celebrate the bicentenary of the Treaty of Paris ending the American War of Independence, and in 1985 Vice-President George Bush wanted to address the Pilgrims, but could not find a suitable date. Several times Lord Carrington told the Pilgrims how difficult it was to think of speakers.[101]

Robert Worcester

Despite all these highly successful occasions, attracting new members remained a problem, although in 1980 the maximum was raised to 800 in order to admit all those on the waiting list, and thus increase the Society's income. It was raised again in 1981, to 850, but by the time of the Annual Meeting in 1983 the total membership was only 760, and in 1989 it was 745. The members continued to be dilatory about attending functions, and there were many discussions among the committee about the need to attract more active and younger members. One of the more interesting suggestions in the 1980s was that the Pilgrims should expand their interests in view of the growing importance of Britain's role in the European Community, and invite some prominent European citizens to speak.[102] But this suggestion was not developed, and the Pilgrims remained true to their Anglo-American purpose.

After sixteen years as chairman, Robert Sigmon stepped down in 1993, and was elected a vice-president. He was succeeded by Robert Worcester, another American, a Pilgrim since 1984 and a member of the executive committee since 1989. A number of new initiatives were already under way by then, thanks largely to the new programme committee,[103] set up by the executive committee in 1990 to organise a more regular programme of meetings, under the chairmanship of Robert Worcester. At the Annual Meeting in 1990 members made various suggestions, including instituting a question-and-answer session after the dinners, or to have panel discussions, and although Lord Carrington pointed out that the main problem was getting people to come to things, many of these ideas were tried out, with great success. It was generally agreed that there should be fewer dinners and more receptions, and to have occasional lectures: in 1992 it was decided at the Annual Meeting to limit formal dinners to two a year, partly on the grounds of cost. The first Pilgrims lecture was at the Annual Meeting in 1991, given by John Ashworth, director of the LSE. Other events included a reception at the National Gallery with a private view of the Rembrandt exhibition in 1992, a reception and lecture at the Royal Opera House in 1993, and a reception at Christie's, also in 1993.

Lord Sherfield

The success of these events led Robert Worcester, now chairman of the Pilgrims, to extend the number and variety of Pilgrims gatherings, and at the same time to encourage applications for membership. The old limit of 850 was soon surpassed, and the limit was raised to 1000 in 1997, and subsequently to 1100. There were two important innovations: after the Annual Meeting on 19 September 1994, at the American embassy, Robert Hunter, US Ambassador to NATO, delivered the first Sir Harry Brittain Memorial Lecture, entitled "European Civil Space". These Annual Meeting lectures had started in 1991, but it was now decided to rename them and dedicate them to the memory of Sir Harry. Subsequent lecturers included Dame Stella Rimington, former director of the security service, on "International Co-operation in the Field of Security" in 1996, Sir Christopher Bland, chairman of the BBC, on "Broadcasting in the Digital Age" in 1997, and Sir Robert May, Chief Government Scientific Adviser, on "Science in the Millennium" in 2000. The other innovation was the series of Reflections lectures, in which a distinguished elder statesman reflected on his life and career. The first Reflections lecturer was Lord Sherfield, formerly Sir Roger Makins, British ambassador to Washington from 1952 to 1956, and a vice-president of the Pilgrims, who spoke at the Royal Society of Arts on 12 February 1996. One memory was of his experiences just before his departure from Washington at the time of the Suez crisis in 1956, when all the ambassadors concerned were kept completely in the dark about what was happening. There were two more Reflections lectures, given by Field Marshal Lord Bramall in 1997, and Lord Healey in 1999.

Raymond Seitz

Unquestionably the most memorable of the ambassadorial dinners in the 1990s was the farewell dinner for the American ambassador, Raymond Seitz, on 19 April 1994. In his speech, which was seen as the best in the recent history of the Pilgrims, he stressed that the United States *wanted* Britain to be part of Europe:

'America's transatlantic policy is European in scope . . . It is the policy of one continent to another. There is a simple observation that if Britain's voice is less influential in Paris or Bonn, it is likely to be less influential in Washington.'[104]

The Pilgrims also welcomed the American ambassadors Admiral William Crowe in 1994 and Philip Lader in 1997, and although there were no send-offs for the British ambassadors Sir John Kerr or Sir Christopher Meyer, Sir John Kerr was welcomed home with a lunch on 18 February 1998. There were other important dinners: Caspar Weinberger, the US Defense Secretary at the time of the Falklands war, was entertained on 27 January 1994 at the Mansion House. Weinberger, a passionate advocate of the "special relationship" between Britain and the United States, strongly criticised those who claimed that this relationship no longer existed:

Caspar Weinberger

'The UK and the US have had, and do have, a unique fraternal association, and it is a fortunate thing for the world that we do. It is not a relationship based on combined military might, or even the common bond of language. It goes much deeper than that, and in fact it goes back to a mutual love of freedom, a mutual willingness to fight to keep it whatever the cost, and a mutual set of ideals . . . The English speaking people are those who have demonstrated time and again that they are the ones most determined to keep peace and freedom secure for our friends and for ourselves.'

Another distinguished American guest was William Rehnquist, Chief Justice of the United States. At the dinner in his honour on 17 July 1995, he spoke about the importance of poetry to the Anglo-American relationship: 'in a larger sense we are bound together by our common language, and particularly by its literature'. Several leading British politicians agreed to address the Pilgrims, including Malcolm Rifkind, Secretary of State for Defence, on 15 November 1994, Kenneth Clarke, the Chancellor of the Exchequer, on 15 February 1995, and John Major, the former Prime Minister, on 20 October 1997. Kenneth Clarke's speech reinforced the message conveyed by Raymond Seitz a few months earlier:

'Britain's standing with the US is enhanced, not weakened, by our standing in Europe. The US judges us in part by the weight we carry in Bonn and Paris. Strong ties with Europe complement our strong ties in the United States.'

There were receptions in St James's Palace, in the presence of the Queen, in 1994, and at the House of Commons in 1994 and 1997, while the tradition of holding receptions at the American ambassador's residence, Winfield House, continued in 1995 and 2000. Some of the receptions were linked to cultural events: the spring reception in 1996 was at the Royal Botanic Gardens at Kew, with tours of the gardens, and in 1998 it was in the Conservatory at the Barbican, followed by the opportunity to attend a concert of American music in the Barbican concert hall. There were also several lunches and dinners with guest speakers: these included former ambassador Sir John Kerr, who spoke on "Britain in the EU: The Perspective from America", at a lunch on 18 February 1998, and Professor Anthony Giddens, director of the LSE, and author of *The Third Way: The Renewal of Social Democracy* (1998), who spoke on "Globalisation and the Third Way" at a dinner on 10 February 2000.

Why have the Pilgrims survived, when so many other societies dedicated to the furthering of Anglo-American friendship and founded at the same time have vanished? Probably the most important reason is that they were fortunate in having such single-minded people in charge, especially in the early days. The Pilgrims – like most organisations – were at their most successful when there was one person in charge, who took decisions. As Lord Chalfont, a member of the executive committee, has remarked, the Pilgrims do not need democracy.[105] People like Harry Brittain and Sir Campbell Stuart were not universally popular, but they got things done. They used all their contacts, they left nothing to chance, they proclaimed the Pilgrims Society to be the best Anglo-American society in the world, and they attended to the tiniest details involved in making a dinner a success. And in the years in between, John Wilson Taylor, in his quiet way, made sure that the Pilgrims thrived. Harry Brittain's two passions were the Pilgrims and the Commonwealth Press Union; John Wilson Taylor dedicated his life to the Pilgrims and the Bath Club; and Sir Campbell Stuart was devoted to the Pilgrims and *The Times*. Wilson Taylor and Stuart were also bachelors, with no other demands on their time. In the later years of the century, Lord Astor and Robert Worcester in particular built on the foundations laid by earlier generations.

Another reason for the survival of the Pilgrims Society has been its role as a social forum.[106] Although many important political figures have addressed the Pilgrims on serious topics, in the end the Pilgrims are under no illusion that they have any political role to play, or that they have any influence on government policy. What is important is that members of the Anglo-American community, and those who are interested in American affairs, can meet in a social context, and as such the Pilgrims gatherings are regarded as important by political leaders. As Raymond Seitz put it: 'I . . . put The Pilgrims in a category different from most other associations and institutions. It's not "official", but it *feels* official. It really is the London capstone of traditional Anglo-American relations'.[107]

The Pilgrims have been able to move with the times. From trivial changes such as the move to black-tie events in the 1960s, to more fundamental changes like the admission of women members in the late 1970s, the increase in informal receptions in the 1980s, and the introduction of lectures and cultural events in the 1990s, the Pilgrims have shown they are not moribund. With a membership of 1100, and a number of new younger Pilgrims, including many who work for American companies in the City, the Society seems set to continue in its traditional role of fostering Anglo-American good fellowship.

NOTES

1 Joseph Choate, president of the Pilgrims of the United States, at the tenth anniversary dinner of the American Pilgrims, 4 February 1913.

2 Commander-in-Chief of the British Army.

3 An Irishman who had taken part in the relief of Mafeking. Later General Sir Bryan Mahon.

4 This name turned out to be an inspired choice. There was much talk in the early years of 'Brother Pilgrims', a much more appealing form of address than 'Brother member of the Anglo-American League', for example.

5 Letter circulated after the meeting on 11 July.

6 Veteran of the Egyptian campaigns, and Governor of Malta 1899–1902.

7 Senator for New York 1899–1911, and chairman of the New York Central Railroad. President of the Pilgrims of the United States 1917–28.

8 In command of the royal yacht *Victoria and Albert,* and equerry to Edward VII.

9 He was working in London in 1902, as vice-president of the Equitable Life insurance company, and played an important part in the founding of the Pilgrims.

10 This was not true. There were fewer than 400 members, including those elected in the United States.

11 In a letter explaining why he had not put forward a suggested candidate for membership, Harry Brittain wrote: 'at present we are not hunting for members, and are limiting their number . . . to men who are distinguished in some way or other, and . . . when one takes this line, the more anxious people are to get in'. (H.B. to Edgar Carolan, 29 July 1908.)

12 Harry Brittain had been trying to get President Roosevelt to a Pilgrims dinner since 1908. He wrote to Lord Roberts in 1910 that he had heard from private American sources that the ex-President would be in England for only a couple of days and had already refused several invitations. He suggested that Lord Roberts draft a telegram that he would send to await his arrival in Khartoum (H.B. to Lord Roberts, 15 February 1910). Despite all this, they never succeeded in entertaining Roosevelt.

13 'The friendship you entertain for the people of the United States is reciprocated by them far more universally and heartily than ever before' (6 November 1913).

14 Harry Brittain subsequently published *To Verdun from the Somme,* an account of this expedition.

15 'Incidentally from our point of view as Pilgrims, it has put the Pilgrims over here up to a very happy pinnacle . . . Speaking confidentially, this move is not in any way too soon. This war has now been on for over three years, and we have had – naturally – hardly any Pilgrim functions . . . We had begun to live on a reputation, which however excellent, was a reputation largely of the past . . . Therefore it seemed very essential for the Pilgrims to strike a new line . . . The press here has taken up the whole subject in the kindliest possible way, and I believe the American correspondents are whooping it up pretty good in America.' (H.B. to George Wilson, 30 October 1917.)

16 'During the period of this Club's existence our very welcome guests, the Officers of the United States Army and Navy, have had an opportunity of meeting very many of our people, but there is one section of the British community which they have not yet seen much of . . . which in the opinion of most of us, is by far the more attractive part of the British race, namely, the British child.' (H.B., letter to members of the Pilgrims asking for the names of their children between the ages of six and sixteen who would like an invitation, 23 December 1918.)

17 Notice to members inviting them to the lunch.

18 The Pilgrims secretary, Mrs Welch-Lee (a New Zealander), circulated the Pilgrims in July 1919 warning that unless there were changes she was sure that one of the other Anglo-American societies 'will cut the ground from under the Pilgrims' feet, and the only alternative will be union with that body or an emasculated existence'.

19 He was elected a vice-president.

20 An example of his tact is his reply to a suggestion that there should be a Pilgrims badge. He sends off a badge, but gently points out that members don't seem to care to wear them in England: 'in America they are more accustomed to these symbols I believe'. (J.W.T. to John Greville Earle, 12 February 1924.) Earle also suggested asking Rudyard Kipling to write a history of the founding of the Pilgrims, as most had no idea when or where the Pilgrims started. This idea elicited no response.

21 When he heard that the American flagship would be coming to Gravesend, in 1927, he wrote at once to Admiral Burrage of the US Navy inviting him and his officers to a Pilgrims dinner. 'The Pilgrims claim one privilege which we hope you will very kindly bear in mind and that is this, that we should be the first organization – apart from any Government function – to entertain you.' (J. Wilson Taylor to Admiral Burrage, 7 March 1927.)

22 Francis Powell, president of the American Club, and Clarence Graff, chairman of the American Society in London, were on the executive committee of the Pilgrims, while Evelyn Wrench, chairman of the ESU, George Mower, treasurer of the American Society in London, G. Warren McKinley, secretary of the American Luncheon Club, H. S. Perris, secretary of the Anglo-American Society, Lawrence Tweedy, chairman of the American University Union and secretary of the American Club, and George E. Maclean, director of the American University Union, were all Pilgrims, and Lord Desborough was a member of the ESU. J. Wilson Taylor declined an invitation to join the committee of the ESU in 1920, but expressed the hope that 'we may always work together in cordiality and harmony for our common objects'. (J.W.T. to Evelyn Wrench, 17 February 1920.)

23 When Sir John Henry, of the Board of Trade, was about to go to Washington, Wilson Taylor asked him to find out from the embassy if any important American statesmen were planning to come to England, and to let the Pilgrims know ('We, as you know, are the Premier Anglo-American Society'), as they wanted to maintain their reputation of being the first to give important American visitors the opportunity of addressing select audiences in Britain. (J.W.T. to Sir John Henry, 17 September 1920.) In 1921 he sent an invitation to the new American ambassador-designate, George Harvey, as soon as his appointment was announced, inviting him to a banquet in his honour. 'It is hoped that the Pilgrims' welcome will be your Excellency's first public function in London as soon as convenient after your arrival.' (J.W.T. to George Harvey, 8 April 1921.) Harvey replied that he had many pressing invitations, but he would make his first public appearance at a Pilgrims dinner, 'in accordance with custom'.

24 It is 'a tribute to our eminence and standing, because all the kindred societies have had to be fought and defeated'. (J.W.T. to George Wilson, chairman of the US Pilgrims, 11 January 1920.)

25 A. R. Burrows, Director of Programmes, BBC, wrote to J. Wilson Taylor on 4 February 1924 about the possibility of occasionally broadcasting speeches of distinguished visitors at Pilgrims dinners.

26 J.W.T. to R. H. Eckersley of the Outside Broadcast department, 26 January 1925.

27 J.Wilson Taylor consulted Lord Grey, who was to preside at the dinner, and received a telegram back: 'Do not know what talking film is. Must leave decision to others. If there is very strong light I shall protect what is left of my sight with dark glasses.' (7 January 1930.)

28 'I am sorry to tell you that we have no dinner in prospect, at present, for the coming season. This condition is without parallel in the last ten years . . . However people may understand that it is expedient to have no meetings at a time when public men on either side seem disinclined to be

eloquent on Anglo-American matters; and my committee are determined not to call our members together unless we are assured that the Pilgrims' standard will be maintained.' (J.W.T. to William C. Demorest, treasurer of the US Pilgrims, 27 February 1928.)

29 'In the opinion of many present Mr Taft's speech on the Anglo-American position was the greatest contribution of recent years on this important matter . . . I am sure that the meeting will result in lasting good.' (J.W.T. to F. Cunliffe-Owen, 26 June 1922.)

30 Colonel Sir James Leigh-Wood, one of the organisers, wrote to J. Wilson Taylor : 'I am a great believer in good feeling being more likely to be fruitful if promoted amongst the younger Americans of the working classes' (7 September 1929). Six of the 1929 team were, in fact, British born, and had gone from the carpet factories of Kidderminster and other towns to work in the textile mills of Worcester, Mass.

31 Lord Derby is 'a splendid type of sporting Englishman who will ably carry on the traditions of the chair'. (J.W.T. to John Rogers, treasurer, US Pilgrims, early 1930.)

32 When he discovered that Wilson Taylor had arranged a lunch for Professor Kittredge, the American Shakespeare scholar, on a day when there was racing at Newmarket, he wrote to say that if he had anything good running he would like to be there, so would only come to the lunch if he could (Lord Derby to J.W.T., 15 April 1932). However, he did turn up to the lunch.

33 He wrote to Wilson Taylor in April 1930, after there had been eight functions in the previous twelve months, to say he thought they were overdoing the dinners, and their value was being diminished. He wanted to confine it to two or three dinners a year for really prominent people (25 April 1930).

34 'We have aimed here as you know in maintaining a standard rather than in enrolling everyone who comes along and of late years have been even more circumspect in our elections', attempting to make the society representative and selective, otherwise 'it would become merely a huge dining club, of which there are legions in London'. (J.W.T. to John Rogers, treasurer, US Pilgrims, 17 March 1933.)

35 'I am not versed in American politics, but I assume there may be some Pilgrims in America and in this country who might interpret the paragraph I have marked in red as having some political bias. . . As you know we like to keep free of politics at the Pilgrims.' (J.W.T. to Robert Bingham, 7 December 1936.)

36 Father of David Ormsby Gore, later Lord Harlech, president of the Pilgrims 1965–77.

37 1 August 1933.

38 When athletic teams from Harvard and Yale came over to compete against teams from Oxford and Cambridge in July 1931, J. Wilson Taylor persuaded Lord Derby that they should have a dinner: 'It is a function that is not largely attended by the Pilgrims, and it is one that costs us a good bit of money to carry out. But I always feel that, among those American men, may be the statesmen of tomorrow, and that it is good propaganda work to bring them in touch with our University athletes.'

39 'This is one of the most important speeches ever made to us, and deserves to be printed in full as a complete exposition of American policy.' (J. Arthur Barratt to J. Wilson Taylor, 9 November 1938.) After the speech was printed in full in the *Anglo-American Year Book*, published by the American Chamber of Commerce in London, Wilson Taylor had a hundred copies of the entry reprinted and sent to new members of the Pilgrims.

40 'We have had an outstanding year and are in very good favour with the Government and the public owing to your guidance – We have never had a Prime Minister in our history lunch twice in any one year, since the Society was founded in 1902 by Lindsay Russell.' (J. Wilson Taylor to Lord Derby, 7 October 1941.)

41 Sir Harry Brittain, as vice-chairman of a government hospitality committee, helped to start the Churchill Club for American servicemen and women.

42 9 October 1941.

43 After the death of the Duke of Connaught, Lord Derby resisted Wilson Taylor's suggestion that he should be president as well as chairman: 'You want somebody from the Royal Family whose name would attract Americans.' He suggested the Duke of Gloucester or the Duke of Kent. (Lord Derby to J.W.T., 28 March 1942.)

44 The committee sat before the war, but the statue was not unveiled until October 1947, in terrible weather. The Ministry of Works had made no provision for the weather, and the guests had to sit in the rain. In his autobiography, *Opportunity Knocks Once* (1952), Stuart says he learned a lot from this, and made a mental note not to repeat this exceedingly bad organisation for the ceremony in Grosvenor Square.

45 When it was suggested in 1968 by George Catlin that the Pilgrims should take the initiative in raising a monument to President Eisenhower, Sir Campbell Stuart was totally opposed to the idea. He told Lord Astor that the government should put up a memorial from public funds, and pointed out that the Pilgrims did not have the organisation to take on such a task. He said it took an endless amount of time to organise the Roosevelt statue. (Stuart to Astor, 9 April 1968.)

46 He decided that after twenty years of arranging seating plans and inviting official guests it was time to pass the job on to someone else. However, after he resigned, the dinner committee was abolished.

47 He was a director of *The Times*. *The Times* devoted several important leading articles to discussions of speeches at Pilgrims dinners: after the dinner for Anthony Eden on 18 June 1952, *The Times* took his speech as the starting point for a discussion of Anglo-American relations. When Stuart was organising the lunch for Vice-President Nixon in 1958, he told Nixon that his speech would be widely reported: 'Here I speak as the senior director of *The Times* newspaper – for what you say on that Tuesday will have a considerable effect on the English public.' (C.S. to Nixon 3 October 1958.)

48 Meanwhile the Pilgrims secretary, Mrs Ada Doyle, was carrying on a frequent and voluminous correspondence with Miss Kathleen Rushe, her opposite number in New York, in the late 1940s and early 1950s, although they never met. This continued under Mrs Stella Field, Mrs Doyle's successor.

49 For example, he wrote to John McCloy, American High Commissioner in Germany, to invite him to a dinner in his honour, telling him that the Pilgrims Society was 'the most important Anglo-American dining club in the world. It is its prerogative to entertain the outgoing and incoming Ambassadors, and no public dinner given in this country is graced by a more distinguished assembly' (4 January 1950). And when he was wooing Vice-President Nixon in 1957 he told him 'this is the most important Anglo-American society in the whole world' (11 March 1957).

50 Lord Greenwood was elected president in May 1948, but died in September. So for a few months the Pilgrims were led by two Canadians.

51 When Hugh Bullock, president of the American Pilgrims, came to England to discuss Pilgrims business, Sir Campbell did not suggest that Halifax invite Bullock to Yorkshire because 'quite frankly he leaves Pilgrims matters pretty well in my hands'. (Campbell Stuart to David Bowes-Lyon, 8 May 1957.)

52 'We now have a waiting list of one hundred. Everyone wants to be a Pilgrim since the Roosevelt unveiling.' (Ada Doyle, Pilgrims secretary, to Gano Dunn, chairman of the American Pilgrims, 12 May 1948.) The membership committee had already decided, in 1947, to limit the number of US embassy officials given honorary membership to seven, as their number had grown to 33.

53 He subsequently wrote to Dulles to try to persuade him to come, telling him that he could 'perform a great public service by speaking frankly to the English people at their most important table about the problems of the hour. You are not as well understood over here as you deserve to be . . . In your long and distinguished career of public service, I cannot conceive a greater opportunity to help the peace of the world, than by accepting my invitation and telling the English people once and for all how vital it is that we must stand together. Only you can do it.' (Stuart to Dulles, 6 November 1958.)

54 Sir Roger Makins did not want a farewell dinner, so he was invited to the dinner for General Ridgway on 14 October 1952. The chairman mentioned him in his remarks, and Makins replied briefly.

55 Dinner in honour of Ambassador John Hay Whitney, 4 April 1957.

56 The historian Helen Cam, who had spent six years at Harvard, thought it so good and unhackneyed that she wanted copies to send to her American friends, believing it would please Americans as much as it had pleased her.

57 Writing to Lord Halifax before the dinner for the Archbishop of Canterbury, he said that the BBC wanted to broadcast it: 'I really think it is good for the Pilgrims and the cause.' And when the American Pilgrims sent a message to be read out at the dinner, which referred to John Foster Dulles's tribute to Eden at the Nine Power Conference in London, he rearranged the order of events so that the message would be broadcast: 'I felt this message in its reference to you was of such importance that I arranged for it to be broadcast at the beginning of the proceedings so that all the world might hear it.' (Stuart to Eden, 17 November 1954.)

58 Campbell Stuart to George Barnes, 1 April 1952 (BBC Written Archives Centre T14/816).

59 In an internal memo De Lotbiniere doubted whether this was a suitable occasion for a television broadcast, even though Sir Campbell Stuart obviously wanted one very much. 'I did not encourage it.' (21 February 1953, BBC WAC T14/816.)

60 'When on one occasion he was under strong pressure from certain quarters to agree to the speeches at a dinner being televised, he insisted on a whole battery of television lights being set up in the empty banqueting room, so that he could himself judge, from every angle, how disruptive to comfort their glare would be. (Much too disruptive, he decided!)' (Tony Gishford, Honorary Secretary, to Lord Birkett, 15 September 1958.)

61 15 September 1958.

62 When Chancellor resigned to give younger men a chance to revitalise the Pilgrims, he said he was delighted to have instituted the 'black tie arrangement', although some of the more elderly Pilgrims were annoyed with him. For the first time since the war, the Pilgrims abandoned white tie and decorations in favour of black tie, for the dinner for Senator Jacob Javitts on 27 June 1967, and this sartorial change became permanent, except for occasions when members of the Royal Family were present. The last white tie occasion was the Bicentennial Dinner on 6 July 1976.

63 'Our new President is splendid, taking the greatest interest in everything. He loves America, where he has been many times.' (Stuart to Hugh Bullock, president of the American Pilgrims, 6 November 1962.)

64 Concerning the proposal that Hugh Gaitskell should be asked to propose a toast at the dinner in honour of Sir Harold Caccia, Sir Christopher Chancellor wrote to Gishford asking him to consult any member of the executive committee he saw fit to consult. 'Campbell, *of course*.' (19 July 1961.)

65 Michael Stewart, the new Foreign Secretary, proposing the toast, said that in his office he faced an enormous painting of King George III. 'I now have the feeling that, after steadily gazing at those features day after day for two months, I have a fuller understanding of the causes of the American Revolution.'

66 They included Field Marshal The Lord Harding of Petherton, Admiral of the Fleet The Viscount Cunningham of Hyndhope, Field Marshal The Viscount Alanbrooke, General The Lord Ismay, Air Chief Marshal The Viscount Portal of Hungerford, and Field Marshal The Viscount Slim. Lord Montgomery was invited, but was in hospital. Writing to thank the Pilgrims afterwards, Eisenhower said the lunch was one of the highlights of his trip, and 'one of its great memories will be my old wartime friends who were sharing it with me'.

67 Sir Campbell Stuart managed to round up an impressive number of leading academics and prominent people in the arts. The guest list included Lord Cottesloe (chairman of the Arts Council), Sir Philip Hendy (director of the National Gallery), Sir John Rothenstein (chairman of

the Tate Gallery), Sir Trenchard Cox (director of the Victoria and Albert Museum), Lord Baillieu (chairman of the English-Speaking Union), Lord Shawcross (president of the Medical Research Council), Lord Adrian (Master of Trinity College, Cambridge), Lord Kilmaine (secretary of the Pilgrim Trust), Lord Drogheda (chairman of the Royal Opera House), Sir John Wolfenden (chairman of the University Grants Committee), and Sir Douglas Logan (Principal of the University of London).

68 J. W. Russell to Edward Heath, 18 July 1961.

69 Henderson to American department, 18 February 1965.

70 He succeeded his father as Lord Astor of Hever in 1971.

71 For example, Helen Bentwich, chairman of the London County Council 1956–7, attended four Pilgrims functions during her year of office, and Mrs Pandit, High Commissioner for India, came to the dinner for Ambassador Whitney in 1957.

72 24 January 1968.

73 Astor's main suggestion, which was not taken up, was that the Pilgrims should set aside funds to enable young people on both sides of the Atlantic to make a 'pilgrimage' in either direction. He felt there was an urgent need to bring in younger people with a practical interest in American affairs, such as scientists, doctors and travel promoters, and that to appeal to a younger membership the Pilgrims had to be brought into the modern world of highly developed social conscience. He was concerned that if the Pilgrims were to continue to exist and to make a real contribution to the Anglo-American relationship, they must be more than a distinguished dining club.

74 The original idea had been to have an autumn cocktail party at the Savoy, where Pilgrims and their wives and guests could meet informally.

75 Among the forty reporters accompanying Henry Kissinger on his visit to England in December 1973 were three women: while their male colleagues were invited to the Pilgrims dinner on 12 December, the women were only allowed in after dinner, for coffee, cigars and speeches, and this was only thanks to the intervention of the American embassy.

76 Letters and phone calls poured in from people who enjoyed this new departure. 'It does seem as if these occasional Dinners with ladies are becoming part of the pattern of Pilgrims functions.' (Lord Astor to his assistant secretary, Muriel Bell, 7 December 1972.)

77 Stuart to Astor, 11 June 1970.

78 Muriel Bell to Lord Astor, 10 May 1972, urging him to persuade the committee to elect as many candidates as possible.

79 Even before becoming secretary, he was worried about the lack of dinners: 'we must keep the Pilgrim flag flying' (January 1968).

80 Chant-Sempill to Astor, 8 April 1974.

81 Those invited included the representatives of twenty American banks which had recently opened branches in the City.

82 Tony Gishford organised this. He and Sir Robert Mayer drew up the guest list, which included Lord Goodman (chairman of the Arts Council), and Sir Arthur Bliss (Master of the Queen's Music).

83 'I told him that his first public speech in England should be before the Pilgrims.' (David Bruce, the departing American ambassador, to the US embassy concerning Annenberg, 28 February 1969.)

84 After a bad start, Walter Annenberg became one of the most popular postwar ambassadors. In his farewell speech to the Pilgrims in 1974, in an allusion to his much-ridiculed rambling and verbose remarks caught by the BBC while filming a documentary on the Royal Family, he said that his advice to his successor when presenting his credentials to the Queen was 'when asked if you are comfortable at the residence, say "Yes, Ma'am" '.

85 Several Pilgrims objected to inviting him because he was perceived to be unenthusiastic about the Atlantic alliance.

86 When invited, he was still assistant to the President for National Security Affairs, but by October he had been appointed Secretary of State.

87 Chant-Sempill to Astor, 29 March 1974.

88 Stuart Chant-Sempill spent a day with him helping him to prepare his speech, hoping to persuade him to talk about the future instead of the past. (Chant-Sempill to Astor, 17 January 1972.) He does not seem to have had much success.

89 Mrs Z. Micallef, Pilgrims secretary 1975–97. (Interview with Christopher Robson, 31 October 2000.)

90 The Pilgrims had hoped to have their Patron, the Queen, but she was at a bicentennial lunch in Philadelphia, organised by the Pilgrims of the United States and the English-Speaking Union.

91 Perhaps recalling the early sporting interests of the Society, the Pilgrims also presented three Pilgrims Prizes to the winners of the second leg of the Transatlantic Yacht Race to Bermuda, and on up the Hudson to New York.

92 Husband of the writer Vera Brittain and stepfather of Shirley Williams, later Labour MP, Cabinet minister and one of the "Gang of Four" who founded the SDP in 1981.

93 This decision was taken after the new Secretary of State, Cyrus Vance, refused to accept honorary membership because there were no women or black members.

94 Lord Astor to Hugh Bullock, 19 July 1977.

95 The first woman to be appointed to the executive committee was Baroness Young, in 1993.

96 10 February 1983.

97 One of his suggestions, which was never achieved, was that the average age of the executive committee should be reduced from over 60 to under 50. 'I do not mean it unkindly, but there are many vital people in their 30s and 40s who may be no less clued up about current affairs and have no less useful or contemporary contacts than some eminent personalities now well into their 60s and 70s or even 80s.'

98 Sherfield to Astor, 1 July 1977.

99 There was some talk before the AGM of electing a deputy chairman.

100 This may have been because of Robert Sigmon's connection with the Ends of the Earth Club, which had its dinners at Claridge's.

101 For example at the Annual Meeting on 30 July 1986.

102 Simon Kimmins, a Pilgrim living in Geneva, suggested having one 'European' dinner a year, to which European guests and ambassadors from Britain's European partners should be invited. (Memo, 6 October 1981.)

103 Originally called the Events Committee.

104 He elaborated on this theme in *Over Here* (1997) when he said that the United States sees Britain as part of the larger Europe, and that British membership of the European Union is indispensable to the Anglo-American relationship.

105 Interview with Christopher Robson, 24 October 2000.

106 Lord Carrington in an interview with Christopher Robson, 11 October 2000.

107 Letter to Lord Carrington, September 1998.

A CENTURY
IN PICTURES

PRESIDENTS

Field Marshal Lord Roberts, first president of the Pilgrims, from 1902 to 1914. During his distinguished military career he served in India, helping to put down the Indian Mutiny in 1857, and in 1899, at the age of 68, he was put in command of the British expeditionary force to South Africa. In 1900 he was appointed commander-in-chief of the British Army, the last before reorganisation in 1904. He never visited the United States, despite repeated invitations from the American Pilgrims. This portrait is by John Singer Sargent, 1906.

Right *Lord Bryce, president from 1915 to 1917. James Bryce, one of the founders of the Anglo-American League in 1898 and its first chairman, had been fascinated by American society and institutions ever since his first visit to the United States in 1870, at the age of 32, the year he became Regius Professor of Civil Law at Oxford. Author of* The American Commonwealth *(1888), Bryce did much to further Anglo-American friendship. Thomas Barlow, a Pilgrim, wrote to Harry Brittain in 1907 that 'in view of Bryce's book on the American Republic there is nobody who has done more to show the real appreciation that educated Englishmen have for the United States'. This portrait (1907) is by Ernest Moore.*

Left *Prince Arthur, Duke of Connaught, president from 1917 to 1942. He was the third son of Queen Victoria. He commanded the Brigade of Guards at the battle of Tel-el-Kebir in 1912, the last British prince to command a major formation in battle, and as Governor-General of Canada from 1911 to 1916 he was the first to be governor-general of one of the Dominions. He made the first of many visits to the United States in 1870, and was said to have a weakness for American women. Portrait by Heinrich von Angeli, 1877.*

Lord Derby, president from 1945 to 1948, and chairman from 1929 to 1945. Lord Derby was in charge of recruiting in the First World War until his appointment as Secretary of State for War by Lloyd George in 1916. He was ambassador to Paris from 1918 to 1920. In the late 1920s Lord Derby withdrew from national politics to concentrate on horse-racing – he won the Derby twice – and on his local duties, spending most of his time at Knowsley, his country seat in Lancashire. Although Lord Derby did not have any obvious American interests, he had been private secretary to Lord Roberts in South Africa in 1900, and he was a close friend of King George V, who was very friendly with such influential Americans as the banker J. P. Morgan, and successive American ambassadors. He was the Pilgrims' first choice for the chairmanship, which he accepted on the understanding that it would not make too many demands on his time. He was fortunate in having John Wilson Taylor as honorary secretary. This portrait is by Sir William Orpen, 1919.

Left *Lord Greenwood, president in 1948. He had been chairman from 1945 to 1948. A Canadian, born near Toronto, Hamar Greenwood was descended from an Empire Loyalist who moved to Canada at the time of the American War of Independence. Greenwood moved to England in 1895, and served as Chief Secretary for Ireland at the time of the creation of the Irish Free State. He was chairman of the Franklin Roosevelt Memorial Committee.*

Right *Lord Halifax, president from 1950 to 1958. Foreign Secretary from 1938, following the resignation of Anthony Eden, until 1940, when he was removed after the fall of the Prime Minister, Neville Chamberlain, he was British ambassador to Washington from 1941 to 1946. This portrait by Sir Oswald Birley, c. 1947, is at All Souls, Oxford.*

Right *Lord Birkett, president from 1958 to 1962. This drawing is by David Low, dating from the late 1950s. Lord Birkett was one of the British judges at the Nuremberg trials of Nazi war criminals after the war.*

Left *Lord Evershed, president from 1962 to 1965. He was Master of the Rolls from 1949 to 1962. Portrait by Norman Hepple, 1958.*

Right *Lord Harlech (formerly David Ormsby Gore: he succeeded to the title in 1964), president from 1965 to 1977. Lord Harlech had been a close friend of the Kennedy family since they first met in London during Ambassador Joseph Kennedy's period in London before the war, and this was undoubtedly one reason why he was sent to Washington as ambassador in 1961. A Conservative MP from 1950 to 1961, and a minister of state at the Foreign Office from 1957, he went to Washington at a time when Britain was trying to join the Common Market, and one of his tasks was to reassure the Americans that British entry would not be harmful to American interests. During the Cuban missile crisis of October 1962, he played a crucial role. He and his wife were also very successful on the Washington social scene. After his return to Britain, he set up Harlech Television, in 1967.*

Left *Lord Astor of Hever, president from 1977 to 1983, and chairman from 1967 to 1977. Gavin Astor, who took over his father's share of* The Times, *was chairman of the Times Publishing Company from 1959 to 1966, when he sold* The Times *to Lord Thomson of Fleet. He was president of the Commonwealth Press Union from 1972 to 1981. At the Annual Meeting in 1968 he outlined his plans for revitalising the Pilgrims.*

Right *Lord Carrington, president since 1983. Lord Carrington was Leader of the Opposition in the House of Lords from 1964 to 1970, and from 1974 to 1979. As Foreign Secretary from 1979 to 1982 he steered Zimbabwe to independence. He resigned over the Falklands war. He was Secretary-General of NATO from 1984 to 1988.*

CHAIRMEN

William MacDonald Sinclair (seen at bottom right), Archdeacon of London 1899–1911, was the first chairman of the Pilgrims, from 1902 to 1913. Sinclair does not appear to have had any American connections or interests, and so it is a mystery as to why he was elected chairman. He was at the same school as Harry Brittain – Repton – but left several years before he was born. He had been a chaplain-in-ordinary to Queen Victoria, and was to become an honorary chaplain to Edward VII, so may have been seen as a useful contact in court circles. This sketch was made at the Empire Press dinner on 6 June 1909 (Daily Graphic, 12 June 1909).

Left *Harry Brittain. As secretary from 1902 to 1913, and chairman from 1913 to 1919, no one did more than he to make the Pilgrims a success. Only 28 when the Pilgrims were founded, he had tremendous energy and a genius for organisation. Harry Brittain was born in Sheffield, and after Repton and Worcester College, Oxford, he came to London in 1897. In 1902 he made his first visit to the United States, where he met President Roosevelt. Brittain's friend Arthur Pearson, owner of the* Evening Standard, *was one of the founders of the Tariff Reform League in 1903, and Harry Brittain became closely involved in its activities. He organised the first Imperial Press Conference in 1909. He was knighted in 1918, and served as Conservative MP for Acton from 1918 to 1929. This portrait is from the* Tatler, *24 January 1917.*

Right *Lord Desborough, chairman from 1919 to 1929. A member of the Grenfell family (first cousin of "Teddy" Grenfell, partner in Morgan Grenfell, part of the J. P. Morgan banking empire, and second cousin of Reginald Pascoe Grenfell, husband of the actress Joyce Grenfell), Lord Desborough was a famous sportsman. He set records for climbing the Matterhorn, stroked an eight across the Channel, was the only man to row for the Grand Challenge at Henley while a serving MP, swam across Niagara, was president of the Amateur Fencing Association, and president of the 1908 Olympic Games, held in London. Chairman of the Thames Conservancy Board from 1905 to 1937, he declined the governor-generalship of Canada in 1921. Two of his sons, one of whom was the poet Julian Grenfell, were killed in the First World War. This portrait is by A. S. Cope (1918).*

Left *Sir Campbell Stuart, chairman from 1948 to 1958. A Canadian, born in Montreal, his ancestors were Empire Loyalists who had emigrated to Canada at the time of the American War of Independence. Sir Campbell Stuart was military secretary to Lord Northcliffe, head of the British War Mission to the United States in 1917. He was managing director of* The Times *from 1920 to 1923, and remained a director until 1960. A member of the executive committee of the Pilgrims since 1919, and a close friend of the Duke of Connaught and of Lord Derby, it was he who was largely responsible for revitalising the Pilgrims after the Second World War.*

Right *Sir Christopher Chancellor, chairman from 1958 to 1967. He spent his career with Reuters, the news agency, and was general manager there from 1944 to 1959. This photograph was taken in 1958.*

Right *Robert Sigmon, chairman from 1977 to 1993. An American lawyer from Virginia, and a member of the Middle Temple, he joined the Pilgrims in 1967. After the death of Tony Gishford in 1975, he took over Gishford's role in the organisation of the bicentennial exhibition at the Victoria and Albert Museum. Honorary secretary of the American Society and a member of the Ends of the Earth Club, he was recommended to Lord Astor as his successor by Lord Sherfield (Sir Roger Makins, British ambassador in Washington 1952–6 and later a vice-president of the Pilgrims).*

Left *Robert Worcester, chairman since 1993. An American, originally from Kansas City, Robert Worcester is chairman of MORI, the market research organisation, which he founded in 1969, and a writer and broadcaster.*

THE EARLY YEARS

Left *Lindsay Russell, principal founder of the Pilgrims. An American lawyer living in London at the time, he was presented with a silver loving cup at the first annual dinner, on 19 June 1903, before his return to New York.*

Right *(Sir) William Goode, one of the founders of the Pilgrims. An Englishman, born in Newfoundland, he had served in the US Cavalry before moving to London as special correspondent for the Associated Press of America from 1898 to 1904. His brother, Sir Richard Goode, had set up the British Schools and Universities Club in Chicago. This photograph by Walter Stoneman dates from 1918.*

J. ARTHUR BARRETT, Esq.

THE PILGRIMS

HIC ET UBIQUE

LUNCHEON to

Generals CORBIN, YOUNG and WOOD

of the U.S. Army.

CARLTON HOTEL, October 15th, 1902.

A souvenir of the lunch at the Carlton Hotel on 15 October 1902 in honour of the American generals Corbin, Young and Wood, who were on their way back to the United States after a visit to Germany as guests of the Kaiser, to watch the manoeuvres of the German army.

The dinner at the Hyde Park Hotel on 3 March 1903 in honour of the American ambassador, Joseph Choate. Choate, a New York lawyer, and a great anglophile, was appointed ambassador in 1899, at the beginning of the South African War, at a time when there was a lot of anti-British feeling in the United States. He was a very popular ambassador, who spent much of his time in England speaking to societies throughout the country, stressing the friendship between the two peoples. At the beginning of the First World War he devoted himself to the task of alerting the United States to the need to enter the war.

Joseph Choate, American ambassador to Britain 1899–1905. He was president of the Pilgrims of the United States from 1912 to 1917. The British Pilgrims held a memorial service for him at St Margaret's, Westminster, on 21 May 1917, at which the Archbishop of Canterbury, Randall Davidson, said that Choate was in the front line of the group of American citizens responsible for America's entry into the war, although it was not for love of England that he urged this entry, but for the righteousness of the cause. Choate died a few weeks after America declared war on Germany.

Music, 19th June, 1903.

RECEPTION.

1 MARCH	...	" Pomp and Circumstance "	... ...	*Elgar*
2 ENTR'ACTE	... ...	" Salomé "	...	*Lorraine*
3 MARCH	...	" Hands across the Sea "	...	*Sousa*
4 CAKE WALK	...	" Rastus on Parade " ...	... ...	*Mills*

DINNER.

5 SUITE	... ...	" Nell Gwyn "	... ...	*German*
6 ENTR'ACTE	...	" Yesterthoughts " " Punchinello " }	..	*Herbert*
7 ROMANCE	...	" Salut d'Amour " ...	... ...	*Elgar*
8 SELECTION	...	" Merrie England " ...	...	...*German*
9 CHARACTERISTIC PIECE,	" Mosquito Parade "			*Whitney*
10 ENTR'ACTE	...	" Forget me not " ...	...	*Macbeth*
11 SELECTION	...	" My Lady Molly " ...	...	*S. Jones*
12 MARCH	... ...	" Stars and Stripes " ...	... ...	*Sousa*

THE RED BAND.   Conductor, Mr. Thomas Batty.

.. Toasts ..

Toast .. .. .. **"The King"**   " God Save the King "
 Miss HOTINE & Mr. STRUGNELL

Toast .. **"The President of the**   " The Star-spangled Banner "
 United States"   Miss HOTINE & Mr. STRUGNELL

SONG ... " Nelson's gone a-sailing " ... ... *Löhr*
 Mr. ARTHUR STRUGNELL.

Toast .. **"The Guest of the Evening"**

SONG ... ... " My Zulu Lu " ... ...*Hoffmann*
 Miss JESSIE HOTINE.

Toast .. **"The Pilgrim's Club"** ..   " The Pilgrim's March "
 Tannhäuser

SONG ... " Long ago in Alcala " ... *Messager*
 Mr. ARTHUR STRUGNELL.

Toast **"The Law Makers of both Countries"**

SONG ... a. " The Rose " ... ... *Johnson*
 b. " The River and the Sea "   "
 Miss JESSIE HOTINE.

Toast .. .. **"Men-of-War,**   " Soldiers of the Queen "
 Leslie Stuart
 British and American"   " The Invincible Eagle " .. *Sousa*

Toast .. .. .. **"The Chairman"** .. ..

SONG ... ..." Ho, Jolly Jenkins " ... ... *Sullivan*
 Mr. ARTHUR STRUGNELL.

The music played at the dinner on 19 June 1903 for George Wyndham, MP, Chief Secretary for Ireland.

"THE PILGRIMS."

INCOME AND EXPENDITURE ACCOUNT for the year ended June 1, 1903.

EXPENDITURE.

	£ s. d.	£ s. d.
To WORKING EXPENSES—		
Stationery	33 3 1	
Postages	15 16 1	
Telegrams and Cables ...	10 1 3	
Clerk's Salary and Clerical Assistance	26 15 6	
Cab Fares	7 18 3	
Boy Messengers	4 13 3	
Accountants' Fee	5 5 0	
Miscellaneous, including newspapers	10 7 4	
		113 19 9
,, MISCELLANEOUS EXPENSES in connection with formation of Club	10 13 11	
Cost of Dinners, Luncheons, &c.... ... ...£459 0 0		
Received from Members ... 340 1 6		
Cost of Dinners, &c., over Receipts	118 18 6	
,, BALANCE—Excess of Income over Expenditure	19 10 9	
Total	£263 2 11	

INCOME.

	£ s. d.
By MEMBERS' SUBSCRIPTIONS	262 16 1
(*Nothing is included in respect of the amount paid by 66 Members, who have been given receipts up to June 1, 1904.*)	
,, BANK INTEREST, *less* Charges ...	0 6 10
Total	£263 2 11

BALANCE SHEET, June 1, 1903.

LIABILITIES.

	£ s. d.
Creditors	2 8 8
Subscriptions paid in advance	137 11 0
Received for Tickets—A/c Dinner No. 5 (June 19)	50 8 0
Income and Expenditure Account— Balance of Income over Expenditure...	19 10 9
Total ... ... •...	£209 18 5

ASSETS.

	£ s. d.	
1 Hammond Typewriter, at cost	21 7 0	
Subscriptions for 1902-3 outstanding ...	8 8 0	
Cash at Economic Bank, Ltd. £170 3 5		
,, in hand 10 0 0		
		180 3 5
Total	£209 18 5	

We have examined the Accounts of "The Pilgrims" Society, together with the Vouchers, and certify the foregoing Balance Sheet to be in accordance therewith.

LONDON, *June 25, 1903.*

HASKINS & SELLS,
Certified Public Accountants.

The accounts for the first year. The only assets appear to be one Hammond typewriter.

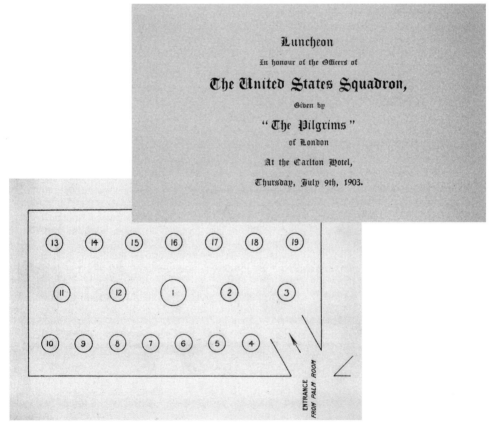

Luncheon

In honour of the Officers of

The United States Squadron,

Given by

"The Pilgrims"

of London

At the Carlton Hotel,

Thursday, July 9th, 1903.

The guest list (with distinctive seating plan of round tables seating eight, and no top table) for the lunch at the Carlton Hotel on 9 July 1903 in honour of Admiral Cotton and the officers of the United States squadron then in English waters.

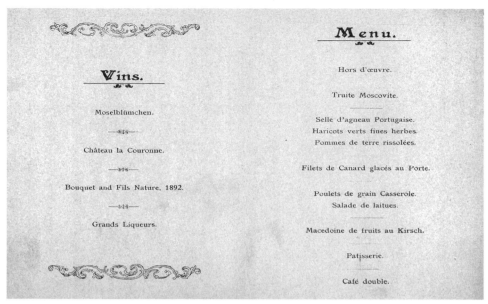

Menu.

Hors d'œuvre.

Truite Moscovite.

___

Selle d'agneau Portugaise.
Haricots verts fines herbes.
Pommes de terre rissolées.

___

Filets de Canard glacés au Porte.

___

Poulets de grain Casserole.
Salade de laitues.

___

Macedoine de fruits au Kirsch.

Patisserie.

___

Café double.

Vins.

Moselblümchen.

___

Château la Couronne.

___

Bouquet and Fils Nature, 1892.

___

Grands Liqueurs.

The earliest surviving menu, for the lunch on 9 July 1903.

The Pilgrims of the United States welcome Sir Mortimer Durand, British ambassador to Washington 1903–6, at a dinner in his honour on 29 January 1904 at Delmonico's in New York. Simultaneously, a group of British Pilgrims met for an early supper at the Carlton, and thanks to the negotiating skills of Harry Brittain, and with the help of a fellow Pilgrim, George Gray Ward of the Commercial Cable Company, they were able to borrow the Atlantic cable for a couple of hours and exchange toasts and messages of greeting. Durand, a distinguished Indian civil servant, was not a success in Washington as President Roosevelt had wanted his close friend Sir Cecil Spring-Rice to be ambassador.

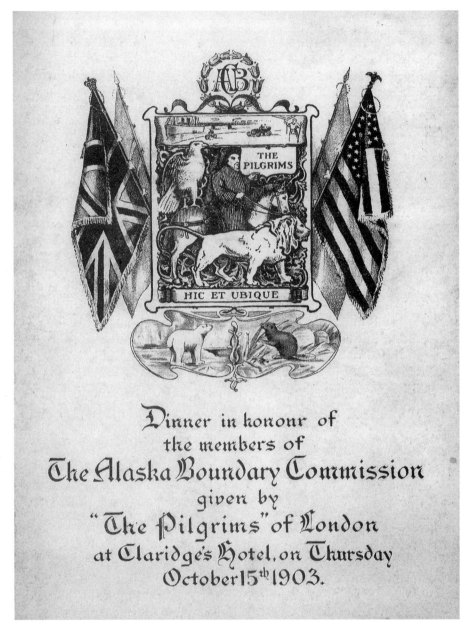

Dinner in honour of
the members of
The Alaska Boundary Commission
given by
"The Pilgrims" of London
at Claridge's Hotel, on Thursday
October 15th 1903.

Following the discovery of gold in the Klondike region of Alaska, and the Alaskan gold rush of 1897–8, it became important to determine the boundary between Canada and the United States in Alaska. The Alaskan Boundary Commission, with British and American members, settled the boundary in London in 1903: this was a significant date in the improvement of Anglo-American relations. At the dinner the Foreign Secretary, Lord Lansdowne, proposed the health of the Anglo-Saxon race, proclaiming the United States and Great Britain as the two great branches of the race. The guests included Elihu Root, US Secretary for War.

The Savoy Hotel, opened in 1889. The Pilgrims first gathered there on 2 June 1904 in honour of Seth Low, former president of Columbia University, and an ex-mayor of New York. From then on most Pilgrims functions were held at the Savoy, and after a few years the Pilgrims office moved there. During the interwar years the Pilgrims office was at the Hotel Victoria, Northumberland Avenue, and the dinners moved there as well.

2ND ANNUAL DINNER
of
"THE PILGRIMS"
in Honour of
FIELD MARSHAL
EARL ROBERTS,
held at The Savoy Hotel, London
June 18th 1904.

The guest list for the second annual dinner on 18 June 1904. The Indian theme is in honour of Lord Roberts, the president, who had spent much of his early military career on the North-West Frontier.

MENU.

Le Melon Cantaloup

Okra

Rondelles Petit-Duc

Darne de Saumon froide à la Britannia
Concombres

Ragoût de Volaille à la Carmen

Oméga d'Agneau
Petits Pois en Terrine   Pommes nouvelles
Ballotine de Caille en Cerises

Emineé de Caneton Rouennais à la Presse
Cœurs de Romaine
Royal Asperges s^{ce} mousseline et beurre fondu

Timbale de Fraises à la Melba
Friandises
Savoury Bâton à la Maréchal

The menu for the dinner for Lord Roberts on 18 June 1904. The first letters of each dish spell "Lord Roberts". This was a popular thing to do at the time.

Savoy Hotel.   18th June, 1904.

Lord Roberts's autograph.

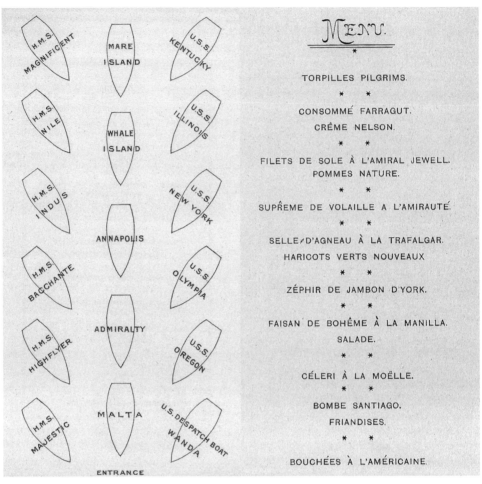

The menu for the dinner on 25 October 1904 for Rear-Admiral Jewell and the officers of the American squadron in British waters. Everything at the dinner, including the menu, had a naval theme: the tables were shaped like the deck of a battleship, laid out in three columns of six ships, each named after a British or American warship. The room was lit by lifebuoys hanging from the ceiling containing hundreds of electric light bulbs. The guests were summoned to dinner by a bosun's whistle, the waiters were dressed as sailors, and at the top table, where Lord Selborne, First Lord of the Admiralty, presided, sat a magnum of champagne mounted on a gun carriage.

The menu cover for the farewell dinner for Henry Clay Evans, American Consul-General, on 12 April 1905. The drawing is by Leslie Ward, famous for his "Spy" cartoons in Vanity Fair.

Whitelaw Reid, American ambassador to Britain 1905–13. A journalist from Cincinnati, Ohio, Whitelaw Reid had been editor and proprietor of the New York Tribune, *the chief paper of the Republican Party. As ambassador, he took over the Dorchester Hotel in Park Lane. His ambassadorship was uneventful.*

The dinner on 23 June 1905 at Claridge's to welcome Whitelaw Reid to Britain. The correspondent from the Queen *commented: 'The Society of Pilgrims thrives in a marvellous manner. Each dinner given by it, no matter on which side of the Atlantic, seems more successful than any of its predecessors' (1 July 1905). The gathering included a number of leading figures from the world of the arts, including Sir Hubert Parry, Sir Arthur Conan Doyle, Rudyard Kipling, Lord Tennyson and Sir Lawrence Alma-Tadema, RA (*Illustrated London News, *1 July 1905). This marked the beginning of the tradition that the first official speech made by the new American ambassador to Britain should be at a Pilgrims dinner. As Alanson Houghton, the departing American ambassador in 1929, put it: 'There are two outstanding moments in the life of every American Ambassador in London – the one when, on his arrival, he is welcomed by the Pilgrims, and the other when, on the eve of his departure, the Pilgrims gather to bid him good-bye' (26 March 1929).*

8   PUNCH, OR THE LONDON CHARIVARI.   [JULY 5, 1905.

"PILGRIMS OF THE NIGHT."

THE magnificent reception and most cordial welcome given to Mr. WHITELAW REID, the recently arrived American Ambassador, on Friday the 23rd June, by "the Pilgrims" and their guests at the banquet (a snug little dinner-party of three hundred *convives*, held at Claridge's) took place too late in that week to be fittingly reported, as the exceptional nature of the occasion demanded, by *Mr. Punch's* special International Representative, who gladly avails himself of the very first opportunity offered of giving, in *Mr. P.'s* immortal pages, some account of this most thoroughly successful gathering.

Claridge's was the humble hostelrie chosen by the gentle Pilgrims for their dining-place, and the arrangements for the simple meal were admirably made and carried out. To feed in perfect comfort some three hundred weary Pilgrims (Pilgrims are always weary) and Pilgrims' hungry guests at various dinner-tables, so that every dinner-table should have its own pleasant little party, and all and sundry should eat, drink, and be merry, without slightest cause for grumbling, is a triumph for Mr. HARRY BRITTAIN, who, true to his name, is nothing if not "a thorough one" in every way; who, though "with heart and voice" he, and others, may declare a fixed determination "never, never, never to be slaves," yet on this occasion is delighted to become a *servus servorum*, and willingly allows himself to be worried out of his dinner in order to attend to his multifarious duties. The introductory melon is being discussed and approved of; our Secretary does not appear. His chair is vacant. Waiter clears away remnants of melons, and disappears with Secretary's portion of the cool, luscious fruit.

The soup is served. When we are half through this, our Secretary, beamingly cheerful, with a lot of telegrams and papers in his hand, and pencils sticking about him, like 'quills upon the fretful porcupine,' suddenly appears and takes his seat as he gives a sigh of relief.

His Guest (sympathetically). Afraid you weren't coming.

Secretary (cheerfully). Lot o' things to see to—(*places a heap of papers and telegrams on table*)—but shall be able to get a mouthful now. (*Commences mouthful, appears much restored. At about third mouthful, a foreign-looking hotel-manager whispers to him. Secretary pauses, refers to papers.*) Eh? Oh, certainly. Yes. (*Foreign manager at his right hand disappears. Secretary is about to proceed with third mouthful of soup when sandy-headed man, appearing suddenly on the scene, touches his left elbow. Secretary turns, listens.*) Eh?—well—I rather think—(*Sandy-headed party whispers with intense eagerness. Secretary considers for a second—then*)— Ah! well—perhaps I'd better—I will.

[*Decides, evidently, on instant action. Jumps up, nearly overturns sandy-haired man, who disappears among some waiters, rushes off, and is lost to sight for another fifteen minutes or so, during which present course is cleared away; and when the third course is half finished, Secretary hurriedly returns.*

Guest (more sympathetically than ever). Can't you get someone to do this for you?

Secretary (almost fiercely). Impossible. (*Genially*) If you want a thing well done—eh?—you know—ah—lamb?—good! now I can get a snack in comfort! (*Drinks a glass of champagne which has been fortunately poured out for him. As he is settling down to the lamb, another hotel-manager, foreign and dapper, approaches him, speaking mysteriously behind a menu-card, as if he were a ventriloquist giving the Secretary a private entertainment. Secretary starts and turns round; then anxiously*) Eh? you don't mean that—(*Ventriloquial foreign hotel-manager, still behind menu-card, explains what he does mean. Secretary starts up, exclaiming*) Certainly; I'll see to it at once.

[*Gathers up his papers, rushes off, and is engaged until [the*

quails have come and gone, leaving behind them but the name on the dainty silken pink riband whereon the menu is printed.

The foregoing will convey some idea of the pleasures of being a Secretary responsible for everything at a banquet of three hundred Pilgrims and Strangers.

The dinner was well chosen, but not quite up to the previous one at either the Savoy or the Hyde Park Hotel, I forget which it was. Intended for a *spécialité*, the "Olio" by any other name would have been a soup. The "*Délice de Jambon Ambassadrice*" was of course intended as a delicate compliment to the Hambassador, which, on the part of the Hambassadrice, no doubt the Hon. WHITELAW REID thoroughly appreciated. The asparagus was served up with Sauce Divine, but there is only one sauce for hot asparagus (if in themselves they are perfect), and that is two table-spoonfuls of cold water with an eggspoonful of salt in it. This brings out the flavour to perfection. Of course if your asparagus be indifferent, and you depend on sauce for its flavour, then I recommend *Sauce Divine*, or *Sauce au diable*, or *Sauce à la burette mêlée*.

Toast-master commands silence for our Chairman. Hearty cheering, and Lord ROBERTS drinks to KING and PRESIDENT. National melodies. After the first toast Secretary BRITTAIN reads out, clearly and distinctly, kindly telegrams from Pilgrims at a distance, including one from Mr. CHOATE which, needless to say, is received with acclamation. Then Mr. ARTHUR BALFOUR, in dulcet tones and well-balanced periods, proposes the toast of the evening, to which, after the enthusiastic cheering has subsided, Mr. WHITELAW REID replies in an excellent, straightforward speech which makes the whole assembly kin.

Lest our enthusiasm should wax too hilarious and our joviality become excessive, the toast-master's hammer recalls us to attention, with a sharp rap (as it were) on our heads, and informs us that now Sir HENRY IRVING (*loud cheers*) will read a few verses, specially composed for the occasion by the Poet Laureate.

The Dantesque figure of our leading tragedian gradually elongates itself upwards, and but for a slight stoop indicative of the gentle bent of his amiable disposition he stands erect. Our first tragedian, or, as he may be correctly described on this occasion, our rising actor, had but to make a brief speech of his own composition which he intended should serve as an introductory prologue to the verses of his "dear and valued friend the Laureate." No wonder that he stooped, seeing what an almost unspeakable burden had been laid upon his shoulders. But manfully he did it. Printed poem in hand, the author as prompter at his elbow, how could he fail to arouse our enthusiasm? Those who had read the verses wondered how he would deliver the line—

"The April-sent swallow circling round our eaves."

But he did it magnificently! Mounted on the poet's Pegasus he cleared the obstacle by a clear foot. Some irreverent *convives* wished to know what the Adams were doing while the swallows were thus annoying their Eves. But to such silly talk deaf ears were turned. In gratitude "our dear and valued" ALFREDO will no doubt present Sir HENRY with a little trifle of his own in Five Acts, containing a fine part for our leading tragedian.

This being over, nothing remained but for Sir GEORGE WHITE, with all his blushing honours thick upon him, represented by rows of medals, to propose long life and success to our hosts the Pilgrims, to which the names of the Hon. STEWART L. WOODFORD and Sir A. CONAN DOYLE were down for replies. For these gems of oratory I was, alas, unable to remain. And so about 11.30 the proceedings came to an end, and WHITELAW REID's entire company retired to their various domiciles. A Big Success!

The dinner for Whitelaw Reid as described in Punch *magazine, 5 July 1905.*

To the Hon. WHITELAW REID.

Composed for the PILGRIMS' DINNER, June 23rd, 1905

TO England's shore hath come full many a guest,
   Seeking for safety, only Freedom gives,
Monarchs dethroned and Rulers dispossessed,
Foes foiled in war, and patriot fugitives.

But never from the young self-governed Land
Hath visitor come, save willingly and free,
With hand outstretched to grasp the outstretched hand,
As brothers greet when one comes home from sea.

Now once again our Western kindred send
One whom grave thought and lofty speech adorn,
Not for whose sake alone we hail him friend,
But for the manly land where he was born.

The April-sent swallow circling round our eaves,
Fresh with the buoyancy of wind and foam,
Thrills us with joy, with sorrow when it leaves,
As though it scarcely knew which was its home.

Our homes be one, wherever we abide,
Ours Yours, Yours Ours, a free-given time-long lease,
Bound by no fragile parchments, but allied
By fearless love of World-embracing Peace.

Alfred Austin, Poet Laureate (as depicted in a "Spy" cartoon in Vanity Fair, 20 February 1896*), author of these verses dedicated to Whitelaw Reid, the American ambassador. The verses were recited by the famous Shakespearean actor Sir Henry Irving at the dinner to welcome the ambassador .*

Right *The guest list for the dinner given on 6 February 1907 in honour of Lord Bryce on his departure for Washington as British ambassador, establishing a tradition of farewell dinners for British ambassadors to the United States. The Anglo-American League helped to organise the dinner, and many members were also Pilgrims.*

SAVOY HOTEL,
February 6th, 1907.

Left *The Pilgrims dinner on 19 April 1907, given at the request of the Colonial Secretary, to welcome the prime ministers of the Dominions, who had arrived in London for the Colonial Conference.* Daily Graphic, *27 April 1907.*

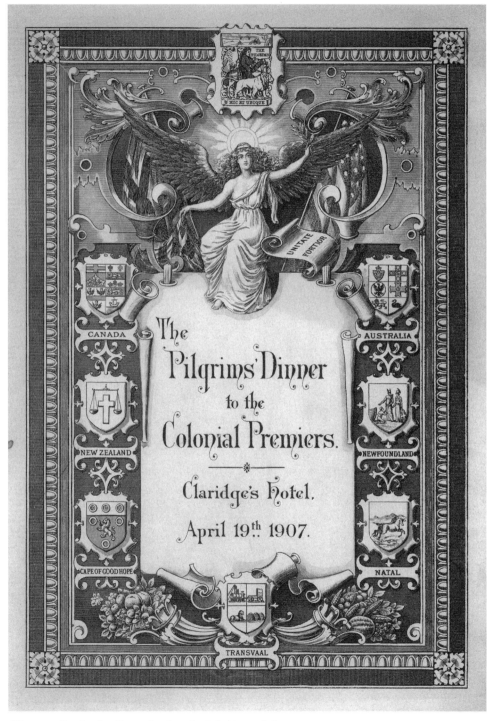

The guest list for the dinner for the colonial prime ministers.

LUNCHEON given by
THE PILGRIMS in HONOUR of
MARK TWAIN.

SAVOY
HOTEL. JUNE 25TH 1907.

Left *Mark Twain, shown here as a Pilgrim with a frog on a lead ("The Jumping Frog" was one of his most popular stories), and a Mississippi steamboat in the background, was in England to receive an honorary degree from Oxford University. At the top of the programme Alfred Austin's verse was quoted:*

*'He lit our life with shafts of sun
And vanquished pain.
Thus TWO great nations stand as ONE
In honouring TWAIN.'*

An anglophile, and a member of the Pilgrims of the United States, Mark Twain believed that the British took peace and order wherever they went in the world, and that the English-speaking countries must join forces to maintain world peace.

Below *The lunch for Mark Twain.*

A number of Royal Academicians attended this lunch for Edwin Abbey, RA, an American from Philadelphia, who had settled in England. Abbey was on his way to install his series of mural paintings in the State Capitol of Pennsylvania. The lunch was chaired by Sir Lawrence Alma-Tadema, RA.

SAVOY HOTEL,
May 12th, 1908.

LUNCHEON

TO

E. A. ABBEY, Esq.,

AT THE

SAVOY HOTEL,

On Tuesday, May 12th, 1908,

At 1 o'Clock.

The Pilgrims had strong links with the Anglican church. The first chairman of the British Pilgrims was the Archdeacon of London, and the first president of the American Pilgrims was Henry Potter, Bishop of New York, while by tradition the Archbishop of Canterbury is always invited to become a vice-president of the British Pilgrims.

For this dinner for the British and American delegates to the International Naval Conference of 1908 (meeting in London to draw up rules for the regulation of naval warfare), the banqueting room in the Savoy had been transformed into the main deck of HMS Welcome. The harbour lights of Portsmouth could be seen off the port bow, with a full moon sailing through a cloud-flecked sky, and a fort on the horizon. A sailor was at the wheel on the quarterdeck, and the ship's bell was sounded at intervals by various distinguished admirals. The waiters were dressed in sailor suits, and the entry of the guests was accompanied by the booming of the admiral's salute.

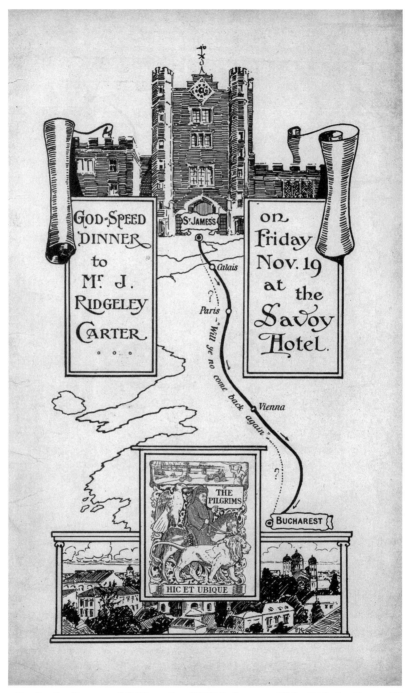

The guest list for the dinner on 19 November 1909 in honour of John Ridgeley Carter, First Secretary, American embassy. He had held posts at the American embassy since 1894, and was about to leave London to become American Minister to Romania, Serbia and Bulgaria.

THE
PILGRIMS DINNER
IN HONOUR OF COMMANDER
ROBERT E. PEARY
At the SAVOY HOTEL
· JUNE 10TH 1910 ·

For this dinner the Winter Garden at the Savoy was transformed into a representation of the Polar sea, with the Roosevelt between the icebergs. The earth, with the American flag planted at the North Pole, rested on massed red, white and blue flowers, while the waiters were dressed in Eskimo furs. In his speech Commander Peary said that the conquest of the North Pole, together with navigation of the air, marked the closing of the book of 400 years of history, and that whatever the work to be accomplished, the Anglo-Saxon accepted no superior. The guests included Captain Scott and J. Pierpont Morgan.

This lunch was chaired by Vice-Admiral Sir Hedworth Lambton, who assured his guests that naval officers were the most peace-loving people in the world, and the Anglo-Saxon race the least aggressive that had ever existed.

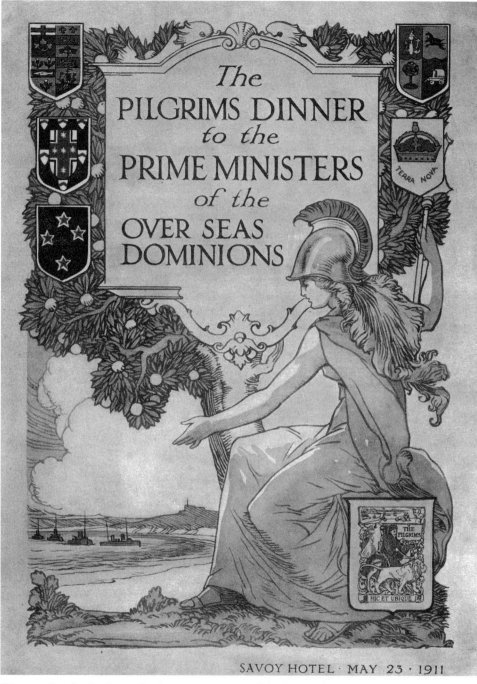

The guest list for the dinner for the prime ministers of the Dominions, assembled in London in 1911 for the Imperial Conference.

The menu cover for the tenth anniversary banquet, attended by 350 British and American Pilgrims. One of the speakers, Herbert Samuel, Postmaster-General, after stressing the importance of good dinners for promoting friendship, told the Pilgrims that the link that bound Britain and the United States more than any other was the Postmaster-General.

Left *Walter Hines Page, American ambassador to Britain from 1913 to 1918. A journalist from North Carolina, founder and editor of the World's Work, he was convinced that peace depended on the co-operation of England and the United States, the two great Anglo-Saxon nations. He was a passionate supporter of Britain during the First World War, and opposed President Woodrow Wilson's neutrality policy.*

Right *The guest list for the lunch to welcome the British polo team back from America. The captain of the team, Lord Wimborne, was a Pilgrim. The first sporting function held by the Pilgrims, a lunch for the American polo team which had just won the International Cup, was in 1909. Sporting lunches and dinners continued up to the Second World War, and included dinners for athletic teams from Harvard and Yale, Cornell and Princeton, the Columbia University rowing crew, and a team of American golfers. When it was suggested in 1950 that the Pilgrims hold a dinner for the visiting athletics teams from Princeton and Cornell, Sir Campbell Stuart ruled that the English-Speaking Union would be more appropriate, as times had changed. Again, in 1970, there was a suggestion that the Pilgrims should hold receptions for American sportsmen visiting England to take part in Wimbledon, Henley and the Open golf championships, but this was not acted upon.*

WELCOME HOME to the British Polo Team upon their return from America, by the Pilgrims, at the Savoy Hotel, Thursday, July 2nd, 1914

Sulgrave Manor, Northamptonshire, the English home of George Washington's ancestors until 1659. This was bought by the British Peace Centenary Committee in 1914 to commemorate 100 years of peace among English-speaking peoples. The signing of the Treaty of Ghent in 1814 had ended the war of 1812 between Britain and the United States. Harry Brittain was a member of the committee. After the First World War Sulgrave Manor was restored by the Colonial Dames of America, and opened to the public in 1921.

The last Pilgrims function before Britain declared war on Germany was a lunch on 31 July 1914 at the Savoy in honour of Harry Brittain. Many Pilgrims were unable to attend, as they were already involved in the preparations for war, but the lunch went ahead, and Harry Brittain was presented with a portrait of his wife, Alida. Lord Bryce presided, and made a plea for understanding with the United States:

'Just as the Thames, which rolls beneath the windows of this hotel, is composed of millions of drops of water, so the friendship of the two countries rests upon the individual friendships of thousands and thousands – I might almost say millions – of persons who know and esteem one another . . . We have with the United States a special kind of friendship which is more than a friendship; it is a kind of mutual comprehension. It is . . . a "League of the Heart".'

—— 101 ——

The American Officers' Club at 9 Chesterfield Gardens, Curzon Street, the home of Lord Leconfield. Harry Brittain organised this club, which was financed by donations from members of the Pilgrims Society. The furniture came from Canadian Pacific liners which had been converted to warships. King George V, on a visit to the club, remarked that the chairs were more sumptuous than those at Buckingham Palace. Originally called the Pilgrims War Club, it was opened by the Duke of Connaught, president of the Pilgrims, on 20 November 1917.

Above *The opening of the American Officers' Club.*
Right *The top of the Grand Staircase.*

A letter that John Masefield, later Poet Laureate, intended to send to The Times, *in which he asked whether it would be possible to establish a means of offering American officers and men hospitality in English homes.*

To the Editor of the Times.

Dear Sir,

During the next few months, great numbers of American officers + men will be passing through England on their way to France, or on missions, or on leave from the front. Would it not be possible to establish some organization by which all these honoured + welcome visitors could be offered hospitality in English homes? I know that various Clubs have opened their doors to them, + that one Club has been founded for them; but a Club offers only a cold welcome to youths fresh from home or college, several thousands of miles from their native land, who have been fighting, in our quarrel, in the mud of France + Flanders. Surely there are very many people in this country who would be proud + happy to offer leave-homes to officers + men of the American Army + Navy. I suggest, that an effort should be made to organize this private hospitality so that it could be brought within the reach of those whom it would comfort and gladden.

French + English soldiers can visit their homes from time to time, + can forget, for a few days, several times in each year, the misery of the mud + the anxiety of the summer; but this solace will be denied the American, who will be, in most cases, a fortnight's journey from any such relaxation, unless our people rise to the occasion. Taking the average period of leave as one week, each householder with one guest-room could entertain forty or fifty officers or men in each year.

Besides this giving of private hospitality, I do not doubt that many

men of the American
would open with th
of magazine & fil
soldiers all through
to supply parrains
would be a very happy
for the supply of ma
worthy charities of thi
(may explain, that in
filleul; she writes to him, knits for him, sends him little gifts of books + tobacco, helps him in his troubles, + makes him feel human in the harsh life at the front. Many English people have been parrains + marraines to Belgian soldiers. It will be easy for them to shew themselves cousins to the Americans.

It is up to us to do these things. Those for whom I appeal will be fighting in our quarrel far from home + friends; many of them are of our blood + all speak our tongue. It will be a great happiness, if our people will see to it, that these visitors who come now as guests and allies, will come in future years as friends.

Yours sincerely,

John Masefield.

Boars Hill.   October 11. 1917.

He was dissuaded by the writer John Buchan, a Pilgrim, who pointed out that the new American Officers' Club already had a scheme to entertain American officers in country homes.

Right *Letter from General John Pershing, supporting the establishment of the American Officers' Club in London in 1917. General Pershing was commander of the American Expeditionary Force in the First World War, and in 1919 was named General of the Armies of the United States.*

AMERICAN EXPEDITIONARY FORCE
OFFICE OF THE COMMANDING GENERAL

August 3, 1917.

Major H. Maitland Kersey,
    7, Savile Row, London, W. I.

Dear Major Kersey:

I have your letter of July 26th regarding the establishment of a club in London for army and navy officers. I think the plan is a most excellent one and cannot say how much we appreciate it. I especially appreciate your continued interest in our welfare.

Please express to the Pilgrims, if you care to do so at this time, my very great pleasure upon learning of what they have done for the Americans.

We are getting along here in about the same way, everybody being filled up with work and with little time for anything else.

Glad to hear the Lord Brooke is coming over here to Paris, where we shall be glad to see him frequently.

With best wishes, I remain,

Very sincerely yours,

John J Pershing,

Left *The Prince of Wales, a frequent guest, with Harry Brittain outside the American Officers' Club. Elected a Pilgrim in 1919, he was guest of honour at a Pilgrims dinner on 21 January 1920 to welcome him back from his North American tour, and he attended several more dinners. In April 1936 he agreed to become the first Patron of the Pilgrims: this caused considerable embarrassment after the Abdication, when George VI became Patron, and the Pilgrims decided to leave the Duke of Windsor off the list altogether. 'I think to transfer him straight away from being patron to the Honorary Members List would be almost an insult to him' (Lord Derby to Sir John Wilson Taylor, 21 May 1937). The Duchess of Windsor's second husband, Ernest Simpson, was a member of the British Pilgrims.*

THE INTER-WAR YEARS

Above *John Wilson Taylor, a founder member of the Pilgrims, honorary treasurer from 1913 and honorary secretary from 1919 until his death in 1943, was also secretary of the Bath Club in Dover Street, famous for its Turkish baths and swimming pool, from 1897 to 1941. Lord Desborough (Pilgrims chairman 1919–29) was president and chairman of the Bath Club from its foundation in 1894 until 1942. An old friend of Harry Brittain, also a member of the Bath Club, Wilson Taylor was closely involved in the running of the American Officers' Club. Efficient, quiet and kindly, he devoted his life to the Pilgrims and the Bath Club (which burned down on 31 March 1941), organising over 100 Pilgrims functions. He was knighted in 1934, on Lord Derby's recommendation. This picture was taken in 1932.*

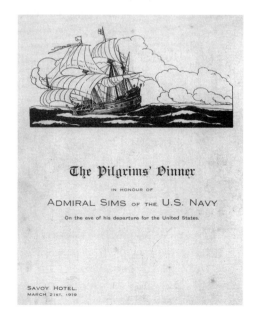

The Pilgrims' Dinner

IN HONOUR OF

ADMIRAL SIMS OF THE U.S. NAVY

On the eve of his departure for the United States.

SAVOY HOTEL.
MARCH 21ST. 1919

Right *The dinner on 21 March 1919 in honour of Admiral William Sims, US Navy, in command of the American fleet in European waters. Admiral Sims had been closely involved with the American Officers' Club. The next time he was entertained by the Pilgrims, at lunch on 26 May 1921, he made a speech attacking Sinn Fein sympathisers in the United States. This led to his recall to the USA.*

John Davis, American ambassador to Britain from 1918 to 1921, and president of the Pilgrims of the United States from 1946 to 1955. A lawyer from West Virginia, John Davis was a very popular ambassador, and a strong believer in Anglo-American friendship. For many years he was also president of the American branch of the English-Speaking Union.

Cartoons by Fred May of some of the guests at the dinner on 28 February 1921 to say farewell to Ambassador Davis (Tatler, 16 March 1921).

A. S. Forestier's The Sailing of the Mayflower, 1620, *presented to the Pilgrims by J. Arthur Barratt in 1920, to mark the tercentenary of the voyage. (The painting can be seen in the photographs reproduced on pages 111, at top, and 138. It now hangs at Allington Castle, headquarters of the Pilgrims.) J. Arthur Barratt, an American lawyer based in London, was at the meeting at the Carlton Hotel on 24 July 1902 that launched the Pilgrims. He was a member of the executive committee from 1902 to 1935, when he became a vice-president.*

Above *A dinner at the Hotel Victoria, probably in the 1920s, as Lord Desborough is presiding. The Pilgrims moved their offices there in 1919 and remained until May 1940, when the offices were requisitioned by the government, and the Pilgrims moved back to the Savoy. Most Pilgrims functions were held at the Victoria during the interwar years.*

TREASURY CHAMBERS,
WHITEHALL. 1.

29th November, 1922.

Dear Lord Desborough,

I am very much obliged to you for your letter of the 24th November.

I shall be very pleased indeed to have the honour to be the guest of the Pilgrims here on my return from the United States.

Yours sincerely

Stanley Baldwin

Left *Letter from Stanley Baldwin, MP, Chancellor of the Exchequer. He was Prime Minister from 1924 to 1929, and from 1935 to 1937.*

At this dinner on 19 May 1921 to welcome George Harvey, American ambassador to Britain from 1921 to 1923, the ambassador, an American Pilgrim, declared that under no circumstances would the United States participate in the League of Nations. He went on to say that the United States had joined the Allies in the Great War solely to save the United States of America. The Duke of York (later King George VI) is on the left, next to the ambassador, with the Duke of Connaught beside him, and the Prime Minster, Lloyd George, on the right. The Pilgrims' painting of the departure of the Pilgrim Fathers is in the background. The Duke of York joined the Prince of Wales as an honorary Pilgrim, and in 1935 the Duke of Kent was also elected, after he was guest of honour at the celebration of King George V's silver jubilee. But after the Second World War members of the Royal Family were no longer invited to be Pilgrims.

The lunch on 14 May 1923 for the team of American golfers visiting England. From left to right: Francis Quimet, the American amateur champion, Lord Balfour (Prime Minister 1902–6), Roger Wethered, the new British amateur champion, and Lord Desborough. In his speech, Lord Balfour pointed out that although it had been played in Scotland for centuries, golf – sometimes referred to as "Scotch croquet" – had only become popular in England and the United States during the past fifty years.

Above *The welcome to Frank Kellogg, American ambassador 1923–25, and farewell to Sir Esmé Howard, British ambassador to Washington 1924–30, on 1 February 1924. Kellogg, a lawyer, and chief government prosecutor of the subsequently dissolved Standard Oil Company, was recalled to Washington in 1925 to become Secretary of State. He is best known for the Kellogg Pact renouncing war as an instrument of national policy, signed in 1928 by 65 nations. From left to right: the Prime Minister, Ramsay MacDonald, the Prince of Wales, Mr Kellogg, Lord Desborough and Sir Esmé Howard.*

Right *Dr Nicholas Murray Butler, president of the Pilgrims of the United States from 1928 to 1946. Originally a philosophy professor, he was president of Columbia University, New York, from 1901 to 1945, and president of the Carnegie Endowment for International Peace from 1925 to 1945. He was awarded the Nobel Peace Prize in 1931. The Pilgrims of Great Britain gave dinners in his honour in 1923, 1930 and 1934.*

The dinner on 6 March 1924 for Sir Auckland Geddes, British ambassador to Washington 1920–4. He was a delegate to the Washington conference on the limitation of naval armaments in 1921, and took part in the negotiations in 1922–3 which led to the settlement of the British war debt to the United States. This was the first time the BBC broadcast speeches from a Pilgrims dinner. These cartoons appeared in the Tatler, 19 March 1924.

Above *The dinner on 21 July 1924 for Charles Evans Hughes, Secretary of State of the United States from 1921 to 1925. This was the first time the Pilgrims entertained an American Secretary of State. Seated from left to right: the Prince of Wales, Mr Hughes, the Duke of Connaught and Ambassador Kellogg.*

2.MORPETH MANSIONS.
S.W.1.

16th January 1925.

My dear Desborough,

    The British Executive Committee for the reception of the American doctors in June have asked me to attend both a dinner and the inaugural ceremony. I have told them that I will do one or the other, but they are waiting, I think, for my brother's return in order to make up their minds which I am to do. If I dine with them, I must decline your invitation. If they choose the inaugural ceremony, I will accept your invitation to dinner unless there is also a Government dinner to which I have to go. I cannot manage more than one dinner.

    So glad you liked the article on Speeches.

        Yrs. sincerely

        Austen Chamberlain

Right *Letter from Austen Chamberlain, MP, the Foreign Secretary.*

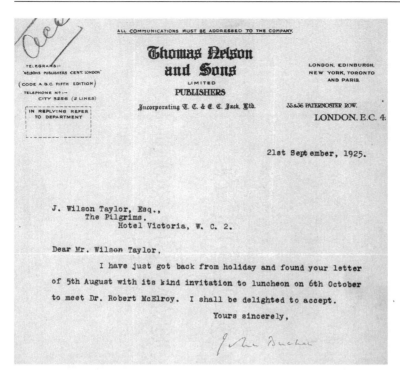

Left *Letter from John Buchan, the writer. Created Baron Tweedsmuir in 1935, he was Governor-General of Canada from 1935 to 1940.*

The farewell dinner on 30 January 1925 for Ambassador Kellogg. From left to right: Viscount Cave (Lord Chancellor), Mr Kellogg, Lord Desborough, the Prince of Wales, Winston Churchill (Chancellor of the Exchequer) and the Marchesa della Torretta (the Italian ambassador)

Above *The lunch on 4 June 1926 for the rifle team of the 107th Infantry, US Army.*

10, Downing Street,
Whitehall.

22nd November, 1929.

Dear Lord Desborough,

I greatly regret not to have been able to be present to-night to greet a friend for whom we all feel a deep respect and affection - Mr. Kellogg. I should be glad if you would convey to him an expression of my warm personal regard, and allow me to join your company in voicing the gratitude we all feel toward one who has made so large a contribution not only to the edifice of Anglo-American relations but also to the foundations of peace.

Yours sincerely,

J. Ramsay MacDonald

Right *Letter from the Prime Minister, Ramsay MacDonald.*

The 25th anniversary of the founding of the Pilgrims of the United States was celebrated on 9 February 1928 at the Hotel Biltmore, New York. The Pilgrims of the United States was founded in January 1903, and the first dinner was on 4 February, in honour of Admiral Lord Charles Beresford, a British Pilgrim who had recently arrived in the United States. Anyone elected a member of the American Pilgrims was deemed to be a member of the British Pilgrims, and vice versa, but the annual subscription was paid in the country in which he was living.

Left *Lord Derby presents a silver model of the* Mayflower *to Lord Desborough on his retirement as chairman, at a dinner on 12 February 1930. Music was provided by a Hungarian gipsy band, and Colombo's string orchestra.*

Right *The Pilgrim Trust was founded in 1930 by Edward Harkness, a wealthy American, founder of the Harkness fellowships. He was convinced that the future of civilisation depended on better understanding between Britain and the United States. Harkness imposed no conditions on how his gift of $10 million was to be spent, and the trustees decided to devote it to the preservation of Britain's heritage, and to social service. The name was chosen by Mrs Harkness, to emphasise the link with the land of the Pilgrim Fathers, and the two organisations have been confused in the public mind ever since. There have always been close links between the two: Lord Evershed was chairman of the Pilgrim Trust from 1959 to 1965, and Lord Harlech from 1974 to 1979. The emblem of the Pilgrim Trust is based on the shell worn by medieval pilgrims to the Holy Land. The Pilgrims gave a lunch in honour of Edward Harkness on 24 June 1931.*

Right *Letter from Rudyard Kipling, 1931. Kipling, who had lived in Brattleboro, Vermont, in the 1890s, was involved in many Anglo-American societies and activities. He was one of the founders of the Anglo-American League in 1898, and the Ends of the Earth Club in 1903.*

Below *Letter from John Wilson Taylor to Lord Derby, 13 June 1932, in reply to a letter from Lord Derby suggesting Winston Churchill to propose the toast to the memory of George Washington at the dinner on 12 July to celebrate the bicentenary of George Washington's birth. Lord Derby thought Churchill 'would do all the historical part extraordinarily well and if we could restrain him from making any caustic comments on present day America, I think he would be as good a man as we could possibly get'. His speech was broadcast live on both sides of the Atlantic. Although Churchill took a great interest in Anglo-American affairs, and spoke at several Pilgrims dinners, he was more involved in the English-Speaking Union than the Pilgrims. A founder member in 1918, he was chairman of the ESU from 1919 to 1925, and deputy president from 1955. He was never a Pilgrim himself, but after the Second World War was talked about as a possible future president.*

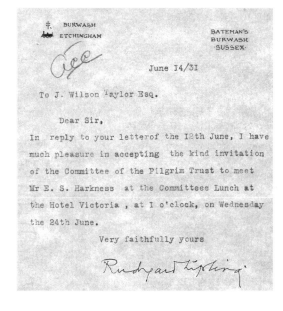

Right *Lunch at the Hotel Victoria on 18 October 1932 to say goodbye to Albert Halstead, American Consul-General in London. The Pilgrims have always worked closely with the American embassy, and after 1925 all embassy officials were honorary members of the Pilgrims during their stay in London. Mr Halstead (left) is talking to Lord Derby.*

Below *Farewell to Andrew Mellon, American ambassador 1932–3. Andrew Mellon, the wealthy Pittsburgh banker, was appointed Secretary to the Treasury by President Harding in 1921, and served for eleven years, despite the changes of administration. Mellon is on the left, talking to Lord Derby.*

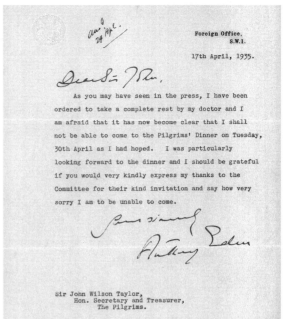

Foreign Office,
S.W.1.

17th April, 1935.

Dear Sir John,

As you may have seen in the press, I have been ordered to take a complete rest by my doctor and I am afraid that it has now become clear that I shall not be able to come to the Pilgrims' Dinner on Tuesday, 30th April as I had hoped. I was particularly looking forward to the dinner and I should be grateful if you would very kindly express my thanks to the Committee for their kind invitation and say how very sorry I am to be unable to come.

Yours sincerely,
Anthony Eden

Sir John Wilson Taylor,
Hon. Secretary and Treasurer,
The Pilgrims.

Above *The Prime Minister, Ramsay MacDonald, addressing the Pilgrims at a dinner on 16 May 1933 in his honour, welcoming him back from his visit to Washington to meet President Roosevelt.*

Above right *Letter from the Foreign Secretary, Anthony Eden.*

Right *Mrs Sopwith, the first woman guest at a Pilgrims dinner, given on 10 October 1934 to welcome her husband, Tom Sopwith, and the crew of the* Endeavour, *which had just attempted to win the America's Cup at Newport, Rhode Island. Mrs Sopwith – seen here with her husband and son Thomas – had been a member of the crew, and although Lord Derby was anxious that it would be a dangerous precedent to invite her, she could scarcely be excluded. Tom Sopwith founded the Hawker Siddeley group in 1935. (Sketch, 19 September 1934.)*

Left *The Archbishop of Canterbury, Cosmo Gordon Lang, with John Gerard, special ambassador from President Roosevelt to the coronation of King George VI, at the Pilgrims Coronation Dinner on 19 May 1937.*

The welcome for Joseph Kennedy, father of President John Kennedy, as American ambassador to London, 18 March 1938. In his speech, Kennedy emphasised that America wanted to stay out of war. He was an admirer of Neville Chamberlain's policy of appeasement, and once war had been declared he sent reports back to the United States stressing the impossibility of Britain's winning the war. He was recalled in 1941. Left to right: Walter Elliot, Minister of Health; Lord Halifax, Foreign Secretary; Ambassador Kennedy; the Duke of Kent; and Lord Derby. (Walter Elliot's wife, later Baroness Elliot of Harwood, was to be the first woman to be elected a Pilgrim, in 1978.)

THE SECOND WORLD WAR AND AFTER

Right *Letter from Joseph Kennedy.*

Below *The farewell dinner for Lord Lothian on 13 July 1939 on his departure for Washington as British ambassador. As secretary to the Rhodes trustees since 1925, he had travelled all over the United States. His speech to the Pilgrims of the United States on 25 October 1939 attracted widespread attention, and in his brief spell as ambassador he continued to speak to the American public, urging them to make up their minds as to what American policy should be. Very popular in America, he died there in 1940. From left to right: Lloyd George, Lord Lothian, Lord Derby and Ambassador Kennedy.*

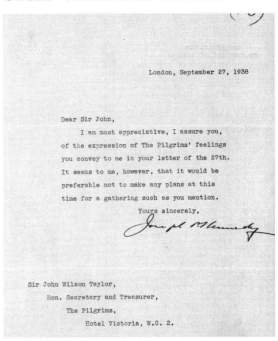

London, September 27, 1938

Dear Sir John,

I am most appreciative, I assure you, of the expression of The Pilgrims' feelings you convey to me in your letter of the 27th. It seems to me, however, that it would be preferable not to make any plans at this time for a gathering such as you mention.

Yours sincerely,

Joseph P. Kennedy

Sir John Wilson Taylor,
   Hon. Secretary and Treasurer,
     The Pilgrims,
      Hotel Victoria, W.C. 2.

Right In November 1940 the Pilgrims of the United States, as a token of their admiration for the courage of the British under enemy bombing, paid for two mobile canteen trailers, each able to provide hot drinks and food for 600. These were to be operated by the WVS in order to feed people who had been made homeless by the air raids.

TELEPHONE
HUYTON 147.

KNOWSLEY,
PRESCOT,
LANCASHIRE.

Lord Derby's letter to Secretary of American Pilgrims

I write on behalf of the Pilgrims of this country to thank you and our American Pilgrim colleagues most sincerely for the very generous gift which they have made to us of 2 Mobile Canteen Trailers.

Your gift will be very greatly appreciated by those who, being driven out of house and home by German bombs, generally in the early hours of the morning, will now get some of that refreshment which is doubly welcome at a difficult time by homeless people.

We welcome your gift not only for its intrinsic value, which is great, but perhaps even more for the sympathy which it shows the American Pilgrims have for their British Pilgrim colleagues; and moreover I think it is a true indication of American feeling towards this country in these very critical times.

Speaking for the British Pilgrims, we thank you from the bottom of our hearts.

Elihu Church Esq.

VINS.

.

Graves (D'Illats)
demi-doux
1933

.

Château Durfort
(Margaux)
1934

MENU.

.

Hors d'Œuvre Variés

Saumon Fumé

.

Volaille en Casserole Bonne Femme

Petits Pois Bleus

Pommes Olivettes

.

Soufflé Paquita

.

Café

Left The menu for the farewell lunch for Lord Halifax, British ambassador to Washington 1941–6, on 9 January 1941. Despite Food Control, the Pilgrims managed an excellent meal.

Winston Churchill with Lord Derby and John Winant, American ambassador to Britain from 1941 to 1946, at the Pilgrims lunch on 18 March 1941 to welcome him to London. A former governor of New Hampshire, John Winant had been director of the International Labour Organization in Geneva. At this lunch the Prime Minister told him:

'Mr Ambassador, you share our purpose, you will share our dangers, you will share our anxieties, you will share our secrets, and the day will come when the British Empire and the United States will share together the solemn but splendid duties which are the crown of victory.'

The speech was broadcast on the BBC Home Service, and transmitted to North America.

THE PILGRIMS.

·

LUNCHEON

IN HONOUR OF

HIS EXCELLENCY
THE HON. JOHN GILBERT WINANT,
American Ambassador
ON
Tuesday, 18th March, 1941.

AT THE

SAVOY HOTEL.

·

RT. HON THE EARL OF DERBY, K.G.,
in the Chair.

MENU.

·

Lord Woolton Pie

·

Poulet au Vin de Bourgogne
Haricots Verts Fins
Pommes Croquette

·

Charlotte Gessienne

·

Café

For this lunch the Savoy served the famous Woolton Pie (Lord Woolton was Minister of Food in 1940): equal parts of sliced potatoes, parsnips and carrots, lightly browned, seasoned with minced leek and parsley leaf, topped with flaky pastry, and baked for 1¹/₂ hours. Created by the chef de cuisine, Monsieur F. Latry, at Lord Woolton's suggestion, the recipe was used all over the country.

Left *The Lord Chancellor, Lord Simon (at left), and Lord Derby at the reception on 6 May 1942 to celebrate the 40th anniversary of the founding of the Pilgrims, and the publication of* Pilgrim Partners, *Sir Harry Brittain's history of the society.*

Lunch on 16 September 1943 in honour of Field Marshal Lord Wavell on his appointment as Viceroy of India. He remained in India until independence in 1947. Lord Wavell is shaking hands with Lord Derby (at right).

The American embassy, 1–3 Grosvenor Square, completed in 1937. Grosvenor Square was the centre of American wartime activity in London. This building was demolished to make way for the new embassy, opened in 1960.

Right *Lord Greenwood, president of the Pilgrims, presenting a bouquet to Mrs Eleanor Roosevelt, widow of President F. D. Roosevelt, on her arrival at a dinner on 4 February 1946. She was the first woman to have a Pilgrims dinner in her honour. Eleanor Roosevelt had been one of the US delegates to the first United Nations General Assembly. Other members of the delegation at the dinner included Adlai Stevenson, who as Democratic candidate was to lose two presidential elections to Eisenhower in 1952 and 1956, and Alger Hiss, adviser*

to the US delegation and president of the Carnegie Endowment for International Peace. He was charged with perjury in 1950, and jailed for five years, after denying before the House Un-American Activities Committee that he was a communist spy.

Below *The dinner for Eleanor Roosevelt. From left to right: Lord Jowitt, the Lord Chancellor, Mrs Roosevelt, Lord Greenwood, the Belgian ambassador and Lord Simon.*

The dinner on 28 May 1946 to welcome Averell Harriman, American ambassador to London 1946–7, and to welcome Lord Halifax, British ambassador in Washington 1941–6, back from Washington. Harriman had been Lend-Lease administrator for Britain from 1941 to 1942, and ambassador to the Soviet Union from 1943 to 1946.
From left to right: Ambassador Harriman, Lord Greenwood, the chairman, Field Marshal Smuts of South Africa, and Lord Halifax.

Letter from Ernest Bevin, the Foreign Secretary.

Foreign Office,
S.W.1.

23rd May, 1946.

Dear Greenwood

On my return from Paris I have been advised to take a short rest. I have arranged to leave London on Monday for one week and I very much regret, therefore, that I shall not be able to attend the Banquet which the Pilgrims Society are giving to Mr. Harriman and to Lord Halifax.

It is, I am sure, unnecessary for me to say how very disappointed I am that I shall not be able to attend. I must, however, take some rest. Please do convey my regrets to Lord Derby, the Committee and the Society of Pilgrims.

Yours very sincerely,

Ernest Bevin

The Right Honourable
The Viscount Greenwood.

Above *The dinner on 22 April 1947 to welcome Lewis Douglas, American ambassador to Britain from 1947 to 1950. From Arizona, Ambassador Douglas had been chief adviser to General Lucius Clay, US High Commissioner to Germany at the end of the war. As ambassador to Britain he helped shape the Marshall Plan. From left to right: Sir John Anderson, MP (Chancellor of the Exchequer 1943–5), Clement Attlee (Prime Minister), the Archbishop of Canterbury, Ambassador Douglas and Lord Jowitt (Lord Chancellor).*

Left *George Marshall (at right), Secretary of State of the United States, was guest of honour at a Pilgrims dinner on 12 December 1947. Marshall, architect of the 1947 Marshall Plan for Europe, was in London for a meeting of the Council of Foreign Ministers. He is shown here chatting to the Prime Minister, Clement Attlee.*

The dinner for George Marshall at the Dorchester Hotel. It was a few years before the Pilgrims returned to white tie and decorations after the war, and the menus continued to reflect postwar austerity: there were only three courses, and South African wines were served.

Members of the Franklin Roosevelt Memorial Committee on the terrace of the House of Commons, May 1946. From left to right: Sir Harry Brittain, B.W. A. Gallanaugh (architect), Col. Clifton Brown (Speaker of the House of Commons), Lord Greenwood (chairman), Sir Campbell Stuart, Waldemar J. Gallman (American Minister) and Sir William Reid Dick (sculptor).

A model of the Franklin Roosevelt Memorial by Sir William Reid Dick, RA. Sir Campbell Stuart was responsible for the idea, and the Pilgrims organised the appeal. The £40,000 needed was raised in five days, with contributions limited to five shillings per person. Sir Winston Churchill wanted a statue of Roosevelt sitting down, but the committee sided with Mrs Roosevelt, who favoured a standing statue in order to portray her husband's courage.

The unveiling of the Franklin Roosevelt Memorial in Grosvenor Square on 12 April 1948 in the presence of King George VI. The King and Mrs Roosevelt are standing in front of the memorial.

Right *Sir Winston Churchill at the ceremony.*

Below *The King and Queen with Lord and Lady Greenwood.*

*The Duke of Edinburgh,
Princess Elizabeth and
Princess Margaret.*

THE MEMORIAL IN THIS SQUARE TO
FRANKLIN ROOSEVELT
REPRESENTS CONTRIBUTIONS IN
SMALL SUMS FROM PEOPLE IN
EVERY WALK OF LIFE THROUGHOUT
THE UNITED KINGDOM WHO WISHED
TO REMEMBER HIM.
IT OWES ITS INCEPTION TO
THE PILGRIMS OF GREAT BRITAIN
WHO THROUGH A MEMORIAL COMMITTEE
CONSISTING OF THE FOLLOWING MEMBERS
TOOK THE NECESSARY STEPS TO SECURE
ITS ERECTION
THE EARL OF DERBY (PRESIDENT)
VISCOUNT GREENWOOD (CHAIRMAN)
SIR CAMPBELL STUART (TREASURER)
VISCOUNT JOWITT (LORD CHANCELLOR)
COLONEL CLIFTON BROWN (SPEAKER OF THE COMMONS)
HON WALDEMAR GALLMAN (AMERICAN MINISTER)
THE EARL OF HALIFAX
LORD KINDERSLEY
SIR HARRY BRITTAIN
IT WAS UNVEILED BY
MRS FRANKLIN ROOSEVELT
IN THE PRESENCE OF
KING GEORGE VI
12TH APRIL 1948

AMERICAN AMBASSADOR · LEWIS W. DOUGLAS

The memorial plaque.

The Unveiling of the Roosevelt
Memorial, *painted by Charles
Cundall, RA. Anthony Gishford,
secretary of the Pilgrims from 1953 to
1964, and treasurer from 1971 to
1975, presented this to the Pilgrims in
1972. As the Pilgrims had no club
premises, the painting was loaned to
the American embassy. Gishford, who
had been on Sir Campbell Stuart's
staff at the beginning of the war, was a
director of Boosey & Hawkes, where he
managed the business affairs of
Benjamin Britten, a close friend. It
was his idea that the Pilgrims should
organise an exhibition at the Victoria
and Albert Museum, "1750–1800:
Towards Independence", to celebrate the
200th anniversary of the American
Declaration of Independence, and he
was closely involved in the planning up
until his death in 1975.*

*Eleanor Roosevelt at the Pilgrims dinner in her honour
following the unveiling of the Memorial on 12 April 1948.
The guests included Princess Elizabeth, the Duke of Edinburgh
and a group of American Pilgrims, and for the first time in the
history of the Pilgrims ladies were invited as guests. The Prime
Minister proposed a toast to the memory of Franklin D.
Roosevelt, and Sir Winston Churchill replied.*

Thou, too, sail on, O Ship of State!
Sail on, O Union, strong and great!
Humanity with all its fears,
With all its fears,
With all the hopes of future years,
Is hanging breathless on thy fate!

In spite of rock and tempest's roar,
In spite of false lights on the shore,
Sail on, nor fear to breast the sea!
Our hearts, our hopes, are all with thee.

THE PILGRIMS

Dinner

in honour of

MRS. ROOSEVELT

on

Monday, 12th April, 1948

at

THE SAVOY HOTEL

*

THE RIGHT HON.
VISCOUNT GREENWOOD, LL.D.
In the Chair.

*Menu cover for the dinner on
12 April in honour of Eleanor
Roosevelt.*

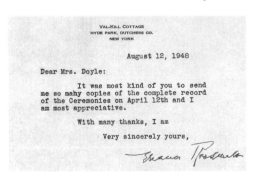

VAL-KILL COTTAGE
HYDE PARK, DUTCHESS CO.
NEW YORK

August 12, 1948

Dear Mrs. Doyle:

It was most kind of you to send
me so many copies of the complete record
of the Ceremonies on April 12th and I
am most appreciative.

With many thanks, I am

Very sincerely yours,

Eleanor Roosevelt

Letter from Eleanor Roosevelt.

Right *Sir Harry Brittain (centre) at the lunch on 11 July 1949 in honour of Admiral Richard Connolly, commander-in-chief of the US naval forces in the Eastern Atlantic and the Mediterranean. Sir Harry rarely missed a Pilgrims event: the last function he attended was the farewell dinner for Ambassador Walter Annenberg on 10 June 1974, a few weeks before his death at the age of 100. From left to right: Sir Campbell Stuart, Admiral Connolly, Sir Harry Brittain and Marshal of the RAF Lord Tedder.*

Letter from Dean Acheson, Secretary of State of the United States.

The dinner on 10 May 1950 in honour of Dean Acheson. From left to right: Sir Harry Brittain, Dean Acheson, Sir Campbell Stuart and the Prime Minister, Clement Attlee.

THE SECRETARY OF STATE
WASHINGTON

April 18, 1950

Dear Sir Campbell:

I am very glad that it is possible for me to accept your invitation to have dinner with The Pilgrims in London on May 10 and am looking forward with pleasure to this evening with your members.

I hope it will be possible for us to get together and discuss details before the dinner as you propose in your letter of April 13 and suggest that you keep in touch with Ambassador Douglas regarding my schedule.

With warm regards.

Sincerely yours,

Dean Acheson

Sir Campbell Stuart, G.C.M.G., K.B.E., LL.D.,
Chairman, Executive Committee,
The Pilgrims,
Savoy Hotel,
London, W.C. 2, England.

Left *Ambassador Lewis Douglas talking to Lord Halifax, the new president of the Pilgrims, at the dinner on 6 November 1950 to mark Douglas's return to the United States. After he lost an eye in a fishing accident in 1949 he always wore an eye patch.*

The dinner on 9 January 1951 to welcome Walter Gifford, American ambassador to Britain from 1950 to 1953. Ambassador Gifford was president of the American Telephone and Telegraph Company from 1925 to 1945, and chairman of the board from 1945 to 1950. The government used the Foreign Secretary's speech to express British support for the United States over Korea. From left to right: Anthony Eden, Sir Campbell Stuart, Denys Lowson (Lord Mayor of London), Ernest Bevin (Foreign Secretary), Ambassador Gifford, Lord Halifax, Lord Addison and the High Commissioner for New Zealand. The picture by A. S. Forestier of the sailing of the Mayflower is under the Pilgrims emblem.

Above *The dinner in honour of Anthony Eden, appointed Foreign Secretary in 1951, was postponed until 18 June 1952 after the death of King George VI in February, because Eden felt that in view of the international importance of the Pilgrims and the distinction of the dinners he should not attend during the period of Royal Mourning. Since the 1920s the Foreign Secretary was* ex officio *an honorary member of the Pilgrims, but this was the first Pilgrims dinner in honour of a serving Foreign Secretary. From left to right: Sir Campbell Stuart, the Foreign Secretary and Lord Halifax.*

Above *Mrs Ada Doyle, who was the Pilgrims secretary from 1919 to 1953, at the dinner in honour of Anthony Eden. She was discreetly hidden behind a huge vase of flowers. She was assistant to Sir John Wilson Taylor until his death in 1943, and for the next ten years managed without an honorary secretary.*

Right *Letter from Harold Macmillan, MP. He became Foreign Secretary in 1955, and was Prime Minister from 1957 to 1963.*

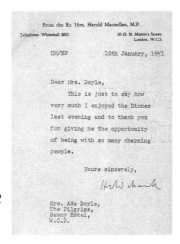

From the Rt. Hon. Harold Macmillan, M.P.

Telephone: Whitehall 8831   10-15, St. Martin's Street,
                                             London, W.C.2.

HM/EP   10th January, 1951

Dear Mrs. Doyle,

      This is just to say how
very much I enjoyed the Dinner
last evening and to thank you
for giving me the opportunity
of being with so many charming
people.

                Yours sincerely,

                Harold Macmillan

Mrs. Ada Doyle,
The Pilgrims,
Savoy Hotel,
W.C.2.

The dinner on 14 October 1952 in honour of General Matthew Ridgway, Supreme Commander Allied Powers in Europe. General Ridgway had been in command of the UN forces in the Far East from 1951 to 1952, during the Korean War. From left to right: the Duke of Edinburgh, General Ridgway and the Prime Minister, Sir Winston Churchill.

Left *Douglas Fairbanks Jr talking to Field Marshal Lord Montgomery at the dinner in honour of General Ridgway. Douglas Fairbanks had been a Hollywood film star, famous for his leading roles in* The Prisoner of Zenda *and* Sinbad the Sailor. *During the war, as a lieutenant commander in the US Navy, he took part in several Anglo-American operations. He lived in England for many years after the war, and was created honorary KBE in 1949.*

The dinner on 18 March 1954 in honour of Dag Hammarskjöld, United Nations Secretary-General 1953–61, and Sir Gladwyn Jebb, British Permanent Representative at the United Nations from 1950 to 1954. From left to right: Sir Gladwyn Jebb, Dag Hammarskjöld and Sir Campbell Stuart.

The dinner on 16 November 1954 in honour of Geoffrey Fisher, Archbishop of Canterbury, on his return from the United States. The archbishop's speech was regarded as one of the best in the history of the Pilgrims. From left to right: Sir Campbell Stuart, the Archbishop and Lord Halifax.

Above *The lunch on 20 July 1955 in honour of Dr Whitney Griswold, president of Yale University. Yale was sponsoring the publication of a new fifteen-volume edition of the works of Samuel Johnson, and it was Sir Campbell Stuart's idea to invite Griswold over to meet the intelligentsia of England at a Pilgrims lunch. The distinguished literary gathering included T. S. Eliot, Sir Osbert Sitwell, Sir George Clark (president of the British Academy), Professor A. E. Richardson (president of the Royal Academy) and Sir William Haley (editor of* The Times*). From left to right: Sir Campbell Stuart, Dr Griswold and Lord Halifax.*

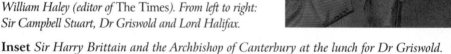

Inset *Sir Harry Brittain and the Archbishop of Canterbury at the lunch for Dr Griswold.*

Left *The lunch on 9 October 1956 in honour of Thomas B. Stanley, governor of Virginia and chairman of the Virginia 350th Anniversary Commission. Governor Stanley is shaking hands with Lord Mountbatten, with Sir Campbell Stuart between them.*

Right *Letter from Harry Truman, President of the United States from 1945 to 1953, responding to an invitation to a Pilgrims dinner in his honour when coming to England to receive an honorary degree from the University of Oxford.*

HARRY S. TRUMAN
FEDERAL RESERVE BANK BUILDING
KANSAS CITY 6, MISSOURI

March 5, 1956

My dear Sir Campbell:

I appreciated very much your letter of February 23rd, and I am sure the arrangements you suggest can be worked out to your entire satisfaction.

As soon as the University announces definitely the offer of the Degree to me then everything will be in the open and we can go to work and get things lined up as they should be.

Sincerely yours,

Harry Truman

Sir Campbell Stuart, G.C.M.G., K.B.E.,LL.D.
Savoy Hotel
London, W.C. 2

Below *Letter from Clement Attlee, Prime Minister from 1945 to 1951, created Earl Attlee in 1955.*

18. 4. 5[.]

My dear Campbell Stuart

Thank you for your letter and kind congratulations.

I shall be pleased to speak at the Pilgrim on June 21st

yours sincerely

Attlee

WESTERN 1617.

La Pausa,
Roquebrune,
Cap Martin, A.M.
~~23 HYDE PARK GATE.~~
~~LONDON, S.W.7~~

2o January, 1956.

Dear Sir Campbell Stuart,

Thank you for your letter inviting me to address the Pilgrims Dinner in honour of Mr. Truman on June 21. I am much complimented by your suggestion, but I must regretfully decline it. Since my retirement I am undertaking very few public engagements, and I would prefer not to add to them.

Yours sincerely,

Winston S. Churchill

Sir Campbell Stuart, G.C.M.G., K.B.E., LL.D.

Right *Letter from Winston Churchill declining the invitation to address the Pilgrims at the dinner for Harry Truman. Sir Campbell Stuart had hoped to get both Churchill and Attlee, the two British prime ministers during Truman's presidency, to support Lord Halifax in his toast to Truman, but Churchill was in poor health, and so Robert Menzies, Prime Minister of Australia, agreed to take his place.*

TO HAVE THE HONOUR OF MEETING

THE HONOURABLE HARRY S. TRUMAN

(*Former President of the United States of America*)

THE CHAIRMAN, SIR CAMPBELL STUART, AND
THE EXECUTIVE COMMITTEE OF

The Pilgrims

REQUEST THE HONOUR OF THE PRESENCE OF

At DINNER

On Thursday, the 21st day of June, 1956,
at 7.15 for 7.45 p.m., at the Savoy Hotel.
The Earl of Halifax will preside.

(WHITE TIE
AND DECORATIONS)

R.S.V.P. THE HONORARY SECRETARY.
THE PILGRIMS, SAVOY HOTEL, W.C.2

Invitation to the dinner in honour of Harry Truman. Truman was on his first visit to Europe since relinquishing the presidency.

The dinner for Harry Truman. From left to right: Sir Campbell Stuart, Harry Truman, Lord Halifax and Robert Menzies.

Ambassador John Hay Whitney shaking hands with Mrs Pandit, High Commissioner for India, at the dinner in his honour on 4 April 1957. Whitney went on to become editor and publisher of the New York Herald Tribune *from 1961 to 1966.*

Letter from Lord Halifax to Sir Campbell Stuart, 23 April 1957. The Pilgrims had always felt superior to the English-Speaking Union, founded in 1918: on 18 April 1919 George Wilson, chairman of the American Pilgrims, wrote to Sir Harry Brittain that the ESU would 'appeal more to the hoi-polloi than the Pilgrims, which is a more exclusive affair'. But the two organisations were great rivals in capturing distinguished visitors to London for their dinners. In 1930 J. Arthur Barratt wrote to John Wilson Taylor suggesting the Pilgrims give a banquet during the Imperial Conference for the imperial prime ministers, as they had done before the war: 'I hate to trouble you on holiday, but we ought to be the first to get them. The English Speaking Union will not be asleep' (29 September 1930).

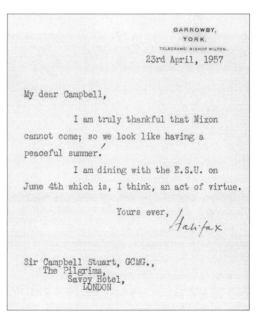

GARROWBY,
YORK.

TELEGRAMS: BISHOP WILTON.

23rd April, 1957

My dear Campbell,

I am truly thankful that Nixon cannot come; so we look like having a peaceful summer.

I am dining with the E.S.U. on June 4th which is, I think, an act of virtue.

Yours ever,

Halifax

Sir Campbell Stuart, GCMG.,
The Pilgrims,
Savoy Hotel,
LONDON

The Admiralty Dockyard, Amsterdam, c.1685, by Abraham Storck, the painting presented by the Pilgrims to Sir Campbell Stuart in 1958 on his retirement as chairman, after 40 years on the executive committee. He chose this himself as a companion piece to his Canaletto, presented by the Canadian government in 1924 in recognition of his founding of the Canadian History Society in France.

Invitation to the lunch on 25 November 1958 in honour of Richard Nixon, Vice-President of the United States. This was Nixon's first visit to England, and the Pilgrims lunch was his first appointment of the four-day official visit. He had flown in that morning, but his plane was delayed by fog, and he had to go directly from the airport to the lunch. Sir Campbell Stuart had flown to Washington earlier in the month in order to talk to Nixon about his speech, bringing with him a list of those who had accepted invitations to the lunch. Although Sir Campbell stressed the importance of the occasion, which would be widely reported, and the distinguished nature of the gathering – 'nowhere will you meet a more distinguished body of citizens than at the Pilgrims table'

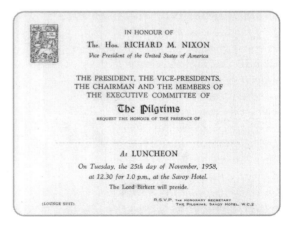

IN HONOUR OF

The Hon. RICHARD M. NIXON

Vice President of the United States of America

THE PRESIDENT, THE VICE-PRESIDENTS,
THE CHAIRMAN AND THE MEMBERS OF
THE EXECUTIVE COMMITTEE OF

The Pilgrims

REQUEST THE HONOUR OF THE PRESENCE OF

At LUNCHEON

On Tuesday, the 25th day of November, 1958,
at 12.30 for 1.0 p.m., at the Savoy Hotel.
The Lord Birkett will preside.

(LOUNGE SUIT)

R.S.V.P. THE HONORARY SECRETARY
THE PILGRIMS, SAVOY HOTEL, W.C.2

(Stuart to Nixon, 3 October 1958) – and despite Sir Campbell's willingness to fly anywhere in the United States to have 30 minutes with him, Nixon did not find time to receive him.

Above *The lunch for Vice-President Nixon. From left to right: Sir Christopher Chancellor (chairman), Vice-President Nixon and Lord Birkett (president).*

Right *Vice-President Nixon shaking hands with Hugh Gaitskell, Leader of the Opposition, at the lunch.*

Left *Lord Birkett (left) talks to Sir Harry Brittain at the dinner on 5 May 1959 in honour of Eugene Black, president of the International Bank for Reconstruction and Development.*

The dinner on 8 April 1960 in honour of Hugh Bullock, president of the Pilgrims of the United States. Hugh Bullock, president of his family's investment banking firm, Calvin Bullock, from 1944 to 1966, was president of the American Pilgrims for over forty years, from 1955 until his death at the age of 98 in 1996. A friend of Eisenhower, he was disappointed not to be appointed American ambassador to Britain in 1957. In 1976 he was the first American to be appointed honorary GBE, in recognition of his work for Anglo-American relations. After this dinner, the Daily Telegraph *correspondent remarked that Bullock had outdone Nixon, at the 1958 Pilgrims lunch, in his generous praise of England. Many people regretted that he remained president so long: by the end of his life the American Pilgrims were doing very little, and the British Pilgrims had little contact with the sister organisation. From left to right: the Ven. Oswin Gibbs-Smith, Archdeacon of London (honorary chaplain to the Pilgrims), Lord Birkett and Hugh Bullock.*

The dinner on 2 May 1961 to welcome David Bruce as American ambassador to Britain. The only American to have served as ambassador to Britain, France and Germany, Ambassador Bruce had been based in London during the war as European chief of the Office of Strategic Services. He went on to head the US delegation to the Paris peace talks on Vietnam in 1970. From left to right: Lord Birkett, Lord Hailsham (Lord President of the Council) and Ambassador Bruce.

Right *The dinner on 18 July 1961 for David Ormsby Gore, British ambassador-designate to Washington. He succeeded as 5th Baron Harlech in 1964, and returned to Britain in 1965. Lord Harlech became president of the Pilgrims in 1965. From left to right: Lord Birkett, David Ormsby Gore and Sir Christopher Chancellor.*

Right *The lunch on 14 August 1962 in honour of General Dwight D. Eisenhower, President of the United States from 1953 to 1961. Eisenhower had been based in London during the war, as Supreme Allied Commander for the invasion of Europe in 1944. He was the first soldier-president since General Grant (1869–77). Eisenhower was delighted to meet so many of his old wartime friends at this lunch. From left to right: Earl Attlee, Sir Harry Brittain and General Eisenhower.*

The dinner on 9 December 1963 in honour of John McCloy, chairman of the Ford Foundation. The Pilgrims had previously given him a dinner in 1950 when he was American High Commissioner for Germany. This was the first speech in Britain by a distinguished American since the assassination of President Kennedy on 22 November 1963. The Pilgrims decided to go ahead with the dinner, but no one from the American embassy was able to attend because of the official mourning. From left to right: Sir Christopher Chancellor, Mr McCloy and Lord Birkett.

Above *The dinner on 23 November 1964 in honour of Alistair Cooke, whose weekly 'Letter from America' was first broadcast on the BBC in 1946. From left to right: Sir Christopher Chancellor, Alistair Cooke and Alastair Hetherington, editor of the* Guardian, *who proposed the toast.*

Left *Lord Harlech talking to Arthur Goldberg (right), American ambassador to the United Nations, at the dinner in Goldberg's honour on 4 March 1966.*

Above *(from left) Lord Astor (chairman), Sir Harry Brittain and Lord Harlech (president) at the lunch in honour of the Chancellor of the Exchequer, Roy Jenkins, on 24 October 1968.*

Right *(from left) Roy Jenkins with Lord Harlech and Sir Harry Brittain at the lunch.*

The dinner on 2 December 1968 in honour of John Freeman, British ambassador to Washington from 1968 to 1971. From left to right: the Archbishop of Canterbury, Lord Harlech and John Freeman.

Left *The dinner on 18 February 1969 to say goodbye to David Bruce. From left to right: Harold Wilson (Prime Minister), Lord Astor and Ambassador Bruce.*

Right *Lord Astor talking to Mr Bruce at the farewell dinner.*

Above *Winfield House in Regent's Park, the official residence of the American ambassador since 1947. It was built in 1937 by Barbara Hutton, the Woolworth's heiress, who gave it to the American government after the war. The Pilgrims first held a reception there on 30 June 1970, when they were given the opportunity to see the Annenberg Collection of French Impressionist paintings (see below).*

Right *The dinner on 28 May 1969 to welcome Walter Annenberg, American ambassador to Britain from 1969 to 1974. Annenberg (left) is talking to Sir Patrick Dean, British ambassador in Washington from 1965 to 1968. Because Annenberg was the publisher of the* Daily Racing Form, *and his fortune came from his control of the horse-racing wire service, a number of guests were from the racing world, including Sir Cecil Boyd-Rochfort (former trainer to the Queen), Lord Wigg (chairman of the Horserace Betting Levy Board), and Sir Harold Wernher (racehorse owner). As Annenberg also had an important art collection, there were representatives from the art world, including John Pope-Hennessy (director of the Victoria and Albert Museum), and Martin Davies (director of the National Gallery). Although the ambassador's speech attacking student unrest in the United States did not go down well – it was very unusual for an American ambassador to attack his fellow Americans in a speech abroad – and although he was ridiculed in the press after his brief appearance in a BBC film about the Queen, by the time of his departure in 1974 he had become a close friend of the Royal Family, and the loan of his collection of French Impressionists to the Tate Gallery made him very popular.*

THE PILGRIMS

*

Dinner

in honour of

His Royal Highness The Prince of Wales

at

THE SAVOY HOTEL, LONDON

on

Tuesday, 8th December, 1970

*

The Rt. Hon. The Lord Harlech, K.C.M.G.

In the Chair

Above *Prince Charles, speaking at the dinner in his honour. At 22, he was the youngest guest of honour to have been entertained by the Pilgrims. For this occasion, because they were entertaining royalty, the Pilgrims reverted to white tie and decorations. As the secretary, Lt-Col Stuart Chant-Sempill, pointed out, 'it should please some of the older members who like the old formality'. In his speech, Prince Charles defended his great-great-great-great-great-grandfather, King George III. From left to right: Prince Charles, Lord Harlech and Lord Butler (Master of Trinity College, Cambridge, and former Home Secretary).*

Left *The dinner on 8 December 1970 for Prince Charles, the Prince of Wales.*

Lord Harlech (left) and Lord Astor (right) talking to Lord Cromer, British ambassador to Washington from 1971 to 1974, at the Pilgrims dinner given in his honour on 11 January 1971 before his departure for the United States. Evelyn Baring, 3rd Lord Cromer, managing director of Baring Brothers from 1948 to 1961, was Governor of the Bank of England from 1961 to 1966.

Left *Paolo Contarini, banqueting manager of the Savoy Hotel after the war until 1961, when he became general manager. For years he kept up a lively correspondence with Sir Campbell Stuart on Pilgrims matters.*

Below *This was the first dinner since the dinner for Eleanor Roosevelt in 1948 to which members were allowed to bring women guests. But there were no speeches!*

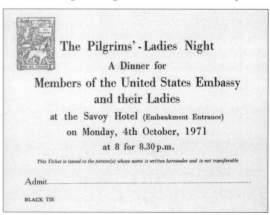

The Pilgrims' - Ladies Night

A Dinner for

Members of the United States Embassy and their Ladies

at the Savoy Hotel (Embankment Entrance)

on Monday, 4th October, 1971

at 8 for 8.30 p.m.

This Ticket is issued to the person(s) whose name is written hereunder and is not transferable

Admit..

BLACK TIE

Right *Sir Harry Brittain,
guest of honour at the 70th
Anniversary Dinner, had
been elected the first and only
"Pilgrim Emeritus" at the
end of 1971. He retired as
chairman of the membership
committee in 1972. He spoke
for 40 minutes at this dinner.*

Below *The invitation to the
70th Anniversary Dinner.*

TO CELEBRATE

The Seventieth Anniversary
of the Foundation of the Society

THE PRESIDENT, THE VICE-PRESIDENTS,
THE CHAIRMAN AND THE MEMBERS OF
THE EXECUTIVE COMMITTEE OF

The Pilgrims

REQUEST THE HONOUR OF THE PRESENCE OF

At DINNER

*On Tuesday, the 25th day of January, 1972
at 7.15 for 7.45 p.m., at the Savoy Hotel*

The Rt. Hon. THE LORD HARLECH, K.C.M.G. will preside and the
Rt. Hon. THE SPEAKER OF THE HOUSE OF COMMONS will
propose the toast of "THE PILGRIMS, coupled with name of
SIR HARRY BRITTAIN"

BLACK TIE

R.S.V.P. THE HONORARY SECRETARY,
THE PILGRIMS, SAVOY HOTEL, WC2R OEU

Above *25 January 1972. The Lord Chancellor, Lord Hailsham, helping Sir Harry Brittain blow out the candles on the 70th anniversary cake, watched by Selwyn Lloyd (Speaker of the House of Commons), Lord Mais (Lord Mayor of London) and Lord Franks (British ambassador to Washington 1948–52).*

Left *Sir Harry Brittain in 1973, at the time of his 100th birthday, with the antique silver ship, mounted on an ebony stand, which had been presented to him by the Pilgrims as a wedding present in 1905.*

Left *Henry Kissinger, Secretary of State of the United States, addressing the Pilgrims at a dinner in his honour on 12 December 1973. His speech, in which he warned that European unity must not be allowed to erode the Atlantic community, received wide press coverage.*

Below *The dinner for Henry Kissinger. From left to right: Lord Shawcross, Lord Astor, Mr Kissinger, Lord Harlech, Sir Alec Douglas-Home, Lord Caccia and Julian Amery, MP.*

Right *Sir Hugh Wontner, Lord Mayor of London 1973–4, managing director of the Savoy Hotel from 1941 to 1979 and a Pilgrim since 1944. At the dinner in his honour on 4 March 1974 at the Mansion House, Lord Astor remarked that it must be the first occasion on which the Pilgrims had entertained their host as their guest. As a mark of appreciation to the Savoy, the Banqueting Manager, Evangelo Brioni, and the Master Chef, Mr Trompetto, were invited to the dinner. Sir Hugh was elected a vice-president of the Pilgrims in 1974. This photograph dates from 1957.*

The dinner on 6 February 1974 in honour of Sir Peter Ramsbotham, British ambassador-designate to Washington. From left to right: Lord Greenhill, the American ambassador (Walter Annenberg), Lord Astor, Sir Peter Ramsbotham and Lord Harlech.

Elliott Richardson, American ambassador in 1975, speaking at the dinner to welcome him to Britain on 11 March 1975. Appointed Attorney-General by President Nixon in 1973, he resigned later that year rather than obey the presidential order to sack Archibald Cox, the Watergate special prosecutor. From left to right: Ambassador Richardson, Lord Astor, Mrs Richardson and David Say, Bishop of Rochester, honorary chaplain to the Pilgrims.

Right *Lord Harlech talking to Ronald Reagan, governor of California from 1967 to 1974, at a Pilgrims dinner in his honour on 7 April 1975. Reagan was anxious to improve his international reputation, in the event that he ran for the presidency, and made a foreign policy speech in which he told the Pilgrims that the communist takeover of Portugal in 1974 marked the first major change in the status quo in Europe since the creation of NATO in 1949. He warned them that the Soviet Union was poised to alter the political map of Europe. Reagan failed to win the Republican presidential nomination in 1976, but was elected President in 1980, serving two terms. His visit attracted a lot of publicity, partly because of his Hollywood film career, and for the first time in the history of the society, a Pilgrims dinner was mentioned in the* Daily Mirror.

Queen Elizabeth, the Queen Mother, at the Bicentennial Dinner on 6 July 1976. The second woman to address the Pilgrims (Eleanor Roosevelt was the first), the Queen Mother was making her first-ever after-dinner speech. She proposed the toast "the United States of America", and General Alexander Haig, Supreme Commander Allied Forces Europe, responded. This was the last time the Pilgrims held a "white tie" dinner. From left to right: Mrs Haig, General Haig, the Queen Mother and Lord Harlech.

Right *Nelson Rockefeller, Vice-President of the United States from 1974 to 1977, greets Anne Armstrong, the first woman to be appointed ambassador to Britain, at a farewell lunch on 14 February 1977. A Texan, Mrs Armstrong went on to be co-chairman of the Reagan–Bush election campaign in 1980.*

Right *Baroness Elliot of Harwood, the first woman member of the Pilgrims Society, elected in 1978. In 1958 Lady Elliot, widow of Col Walter Elliot, a Conservative Cabinet minister in the 1930s, was on the first list of life peers. She was a very active member of the House of Lords, making 135 speeches. She also represented Britain at the United Nations in the 1950s. Her half-sister Margot was married to H. H. Asquith, Prime Minister 1908–16, and while staying with her as a child she whacked the suffragettes demonstrating outside 10 Downing Street with her teddy bear.*

Below *The dinner at Goldsmiths' Hall on 29 November 1978 in honour of James Schlesinger, Secretary of Energy of the United States.*

Right *Sir Robert Mayer, CH, at the dinner on 29 November 1978. A Pilgrim since 1954, Sir Robert was one of those who suggested to the new chairman, Lord Astor, ways of revitalising the society. He wrote to Lord Astor: 'I venture to think that among elements missing for vitalizing the Pilgrims are youth and labour; also that the present monastic basis might profit from modernization, i.e. the inclusion of women.' Sir Robert, founder of the Robert Mayer Concerts for Children, and "Youth and Music", died in 1985 at the age of 105.*

Below *The Pilgrims reception at St James's Palace on 21 March 1979 in honour of the Queen and the Duke of Edinburgh. From left to right: Lord Astor, HM the Queen, Lord and Lady Sherfield and Sir Hugh Wontner.*

Sir Nicholas Henderson (right), British ambassador-designate to Washington, at a reception in his honour at Fishmongers' Hall on 9 July 1979, with Lady Henderson and Lord Astor. As chairman and then president, Lord Astor attempted to revitalise the Pilgrims, and one of his ideas was to follow the lead of the Pilgrims of the United States and replace some of the formal dinners with receptions. This was the third reception to be held in 1979.

Right *Lt-Col Stuart Chant-Sempill and his wife, Lady Sempill, at the reception at St James's Palace. Chant-Sempill was honorary secretary of the Pilgrims from 1968 until his death in 1991. A public relations consultant, he had served as a public relations officer at SHAPE (Supreme Headquarters Allied Powers Europe) from 1951 to 1957.*

Right *A letter from the Prime Minister, Margaret Thatcher, concerning the dinner to be held in her honour on 29 January 1981. Her speech, in which she stressed Britain's eagerness to help revive the alliance between the United States and Europe, was widely reported.*

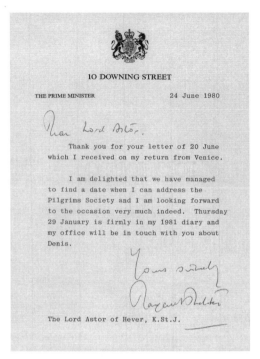

10 DOWNING STREET

THE PRIME MINISTER   24 June 1980

Dear Lord Astor,

Thank you for your letter of 20 June which I received on my return from Venice.

I am delighted that we have managed to find a date when I can address the Pilgrims Society and I am looking forward to the occasion very much indeed. Thursday 29 January is firmly in my 1981 diary and my office will be in touch with you about Denis.

Yours sincerely
Margaret Thatcher

The Lord Astor of Hever, K.St.J.

Below *Sir Nicholas Henderson (left), British ambassador in Washington from 1979 to 1982, and Sir Anthony Parsons, British ambassador at the United Nations from 1979 to 1982, at the dinner in their honour on 25 October 1982.*

The dinner on 11 July 1983 in honour of George Thomas, Speaker of the House of Commons from 1976 to 1983. Although since 1953 the Speaker had always been invited to become a vice-president, this was the first Pilgrims dinner in honour of a Speaker. George Thomas, Labour MP for Cardiff from 1945 to 1983, was created Viscount Tonypandy of Rhondda in 1983. From left to right: Mrs Weatherill, Bernard Weatherill (the new Speaker), unknown guest, Lord Astor and George Thomas.

Right *Lady Falkender with George Thomas at the dinner on 11 July 1983. Lady Falkender, formerly Mrs Marcia Williams, was Private and Political Secretary to Harold Wilson (Prime Minister 1964–70, and 1970–4), from 1956 to 1983.*

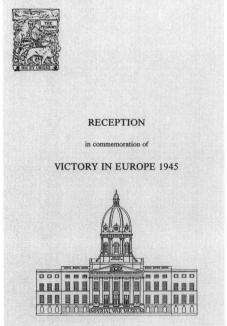

The dinner on 16 January 1984 in honour of Charles Price, American ambassador to Britain from 1984 to 1989. Ambassador Price (left), from Kansas City, is seen here talking to Lord Carrington.

Left *The Pilgrims held a reception at the Imperial War Museum on 2 May 1985 to commemorate the 40th anniversary of Victory in Europe.*

The lunch at Claridge's on 10 December 1985 in honour of George Schultz, Secretary of State of the United States. Mr Schultz spoke about the Middle East, and ruled out a role for the PLO in the Middle East peace process until it recognised the right of Israel to exist.

Right *Guests at the lunch for George Schultz.*

Left *The dinner on 13 February 1986 in honour of the Foreign Secretary, Sir Geoffrey Howe. Sir Geoffrey (left) was Foreign Secretary from 1983 to 1989. He is talking to Lord Carrington.*

Below *The dinner on 10 July 1986 in honour of Sir Anthony Acland, former head of the Diplomatic Service, and British ambassador-designate to Washington, where he served from 1986 to 1991. From left to right: Robert Sigmon, Sir Anthony Acland and Lord Carrington.*

Right *Sir Anthony Acland with Lord Caccia at the dinner on 10 July 1986. As Sir Harold Caccia, Lord Caccia was British ambassador in Washington from 1956 to 1962.*

Below *The Rt Rev. David Say, Bishop of Rochester, and honorary chaplain to the Pilgrims since 1968, with Robert Sigmon and Sir Anthony Acland at the dinner on 10 July 1986.*

The dinner on 18 May 1989 in honour of Henry Catto, American ambassador to Britain from 1989 to 1991. Ambassador Catto, a Texan, went on to become director of the United States Information Agency in 1991. From left to right: Robert Sigmon, Ambassador Catto and Lord Carrington.

On 5 May 1992 the Pilgrims held a reception at the National Gallery, including a private view of the exhibition "Rembrandt: The Master and his Workshop". This was a new departure for the Pilgrims, the first of several cultural events during the 1990s, including a lecture by Jeremy Isaacs at the Royal Opera House in 1992, a tour of the Royal Botanic Gardens at Kew in 1996, a concert of American music at the Barbican in 1998, and an outing to Greenwich in 2000.

Above *This Calman cartoon, "Toasting the President", could have been sketched at a Pilgrims dinner, especially in view of the "Pellegrinos" bearing in the food.* Calman's Savoy Sketchbook, 1994; *drawing by Mel Calman.*

Right *Caspar Weinberger, Secretary of Defense of the United States from 1981 to 1987, speaking at the dinner in his honour on 27 January 1994 at the Mansion House, at which Lady Brittain was an honoured guest.*

Left *Raymond Seitz, previously Minister at the American embassy from 1984 to 1989, and American ambassador to Britain from 1991 to 1994, the first career diplomat to hold the ambassadorship. Claridge's was closed to the public for only the third time in its history for the Pilgrims farewell dinner for Seitz.*

Right *Lord Sherfield, a vice-president of the Pilgrims. As Sir Roger Makins he was British ambassador in Washington from 1953 to 1956. His return coincided with the Suez crisis, a bad period in the history of Anglo-American relations. He managed to escape without either a farewell or welcome-home dinner (although he was welcomed by the American Pilgrims on 2 February 1953). His wife was American, daughter of Dwight Davis, founder of the Davis Cup. On 12 February 1996, at the age of 92, Lord Sherfield gave the first of the Pilgrims series of Reflections lectures.*

The dinner on 18 November 1996 in honour of Field Marshal Sir Peter Inge, Chief of the Defence Staff.

The visit to Greenwich on 16 June 2000. A group of Pilgrims went by boat to the National Maritime Museum, and had lunch in the Upper Painted Hall of the Royal Naval College. Sir David Hardy, a Pilgrim and chairman of the trustees of the National Maritime Museum, is addressing the gathering.

Allington Castle near Maidstone in Kent, headquarters of the Pilgrims of Great Britain. The Pilgrims archives have been kept here since 1998.

APPENDIX

PRESIDENTS

1902–14	Field Marshal The Earl Roberts	1950–58	The Earl of Halifax
1915–17	Viscount Bryce	1958–62	Lord Birkett
1917–42	Field Marshal HRH The Duke of Connaught	1962–5	Lord Evershed
		1965–77	Lord Harlech
1945–8	The Earl of Derby	1977–83	Lord Astor of Hever
1948	Viscount Greenwood	1983–	Lord Carrington

CHAIRMEN OF THE EXECUTIVE COMMITTEE

1902–13	The Venerable Archdeacon William MacDonald Sinclair	1948–58	Sir Campbell Stuart
		1958–67	Sir Christopher Chancellor
1913–19	Harry Brittain	1967–77	Lord Astor of Hever
1919–29	Lord Desborough	1977–93	Robert Sigmon
1929–45	The Earl of Derby	1993–	Robert Worcester
1945–8	Viscount Greenwood		

HONORARY SECRETARIES

1902–13	Harry Brittain	1966–7	John Ackroyd
1919–43	(Sir) John Wilson Taylor	1968–91	Lt-Col Stuart Chant-Sempill
1953–64	Anthony Gishford	1991–	Peter Barton

HONORARY TREASURERS

1902–3	Sir William Bell	1944–71	Sir Julian Crossley
1903–7	Stephen Gambrill	1971–5	Anthony Gishford
1908–12	Sir William Bell	1975–81	John Corbett
1913–43	(Sir) John Wilson Taylor	1982–97	Sir James Butler
1943	Sir John Caulcott	1997–	Lord Sharman

SECRETARIES

1905–19	Mrs M. E. Welsh Lee (formerly Miss M. E. Elliott Wright, to c. 1917)	1963–70	Miss Mary Burfield
		1971–5	Mrs Muriel Bell
		1975–97	Mrs Z. Micallef (formerly Mrs Soutry, to 1978)
1919–53	Mrs Ada Doyle		
1954–62	Mrs Stella Field	1997–9	Mrs Jan Dennett
1962–3	Miss Hilda Wilson	1999–	Mrs Tessa Wells

BRITISH AMBASSADORS TO WASHINGTON

1902–3	Michael Herbert	1956–61	Sir Harold Caccia
1903–6	Sir Mortimer Durand	1961–5	David Ormsby Gore (Lord
1907–13	Sir James Bryce		Harlech from 1964)
1913–18	Sir Cecil Spring-Rice	1965–8	Sir Patrick Dean
1918–19	Lord Reading	1968–71	John Freeman
1919	Sir Edward Grey	1971–4	Lord Cromer
1920–4	Sir Auckland Geddes	1974–7	Sir Peter Ramsbotham
1924–30	Sir Esmé Howard	1977–9	Peter Jay
1930–9	Sir Ronald Lindsay	1979–82	Sir Nicholas Henderson
1939–40	Lord Lothian	1983–6	Sir Oliver Wright
1941–6	Lord Halifax	1986–91	Sir Anthony Acland
1946–8	Lord Inverchapel	1991–5	Sir Robin Renwick
1948–52	Sir Oliver Franks	1995–7	Sir John Kerr
1952–6	Sir Roger Makins	1997–	Sir Christopher Meyer

US AMBASSADORS TO THE COURT OF ST JAMES

1899–1905	Joseph Choate	1953–7	Winthrop Aldrich
1905–13	Whitelaw Reid	1957–61	John Hay Whitney
1913–18	Walter Hines Page	1961–9	David Bruce
1918–21	John Davis	1969–74	Walter Annenberg
1921–3	George Harvey	1975–6	Elliott Richardson
1923–5	Frank Kellogg	1976–7	Anne Armstrong
1925–9	Alanson Houghton	1977–81	Kingman Brewster
1929–32	General Charles Dawes	1981–3	John Louis
1932–3	Andrew Mellon	1984–9	Charles Price
1933–8	Robert Worth Bingham	1989–91	Henry Catto
1938–41	Joseph Kennedy	1991–4	Raymond Seitz
1941–6	John Winant	1994–7	Admiral William Crowe
1946–7	Averell Harriman	1997–2001	Philip Lader
1947–50	Lewis Douglas	2001–	William Farish
1950–3	Walter Gifford		

THE SIR HARRY BRITTAIN MEMORIAL LECTURES

1994
Robert Hunter
US Permanent Representative on the North Atlantic Council
"European Civil Space"

1995
Sir Crispin Tickell
British Permanent Representative to the United Nations 1987–90
"Greenery and Governance"

1996
Dame Stella Rimington
Director-General of the Security Service 1990–6
"International Co-operation in the Field of Security with Special
Reference to Terrorism"

1997
Sir Christopher Bland
Chairman of the BBC
"Broadcasting in the Digital Age: Lessons to and from America"

1998
Lord Puttnam
Film producer, and Chairman of Columbia Pictures 1986–8
"The Virtues and Vices of the Information Technology Revolution"

1999
Felix Rohatyn
United States ambassador to France
"Diplomacy and Globalisation in the 21st Century"

2000
Sir Robert May
Chief Government Scientific Adviser
"Science in the Millennium"

2001
Sir John Stevens
Commissioner of the Metropolitan Police
"The Challenges of Policing a Modern City"

LIST OF MEMBERS IN 1903

italics = American member
+ = member of the executive committee

Honorary members

The American ambassador to Britain

The British ambassador to the United
States

Members

Aberdeen, The Earl of

Abbott, Walter (New York)

Adams, Frederic T. (New York)

Adams, Thatcher M. (New York)

Agius, Edward T.

Alexander, James W. (New York)

Anderson, A. A.

Anderson, J.

Appleton, Sidney

Astor, John Jacob (New York)

Atkinson, John

Avery, S. P. (New York City)

Bacon, Cleveland F. (New York)

Bacon, Daniel (New York)

Baker, George F.

+ *Barratt, J. Arthur*

Bartlett, Philip G. (New York)

Beddall, Edward K. (New York)

Bell, A. P. (New York)

Bell, C. F. Moberly

Bell, Keble

Bellamy, Dr Russell (New York)

Bellmont, Hon. August (New York)

Benedict, H. H. (New York)

Beresford, Vice-Admiral Lord Charles

Bertron, Samuel Reading (New York)

Berwind, Edward J. (New York)

Blair, James L. (New York)

Bliss, Hon. Cornelius N. (New York)

Bliss, Frank E.

Blunt, W. W.

Bonynge, C. W.

Bookstaver, H. W. (New York)

Borwick, G.

Boyd, C. W.

Boyle, J.

Brassey, Lord

+Brittain, Harry E. V.

Broad, John

Brooke-Hitching, Alderman Sir T. H.

Brooks, Sydney

Brown, S. Stanley

Browne, Flint

Budd, J. L.

Burn, M. James

Burrows, E. H.

Burt, Charles W. (Kentucky)

Caldwell, Alexander (New York)

Calhoun, John C. (New York)

Cameron, Sir Ewen

Carolan, Edgar A.

Carson, William E. (New York)

Carter, James C. (New York)

Cassatt, Major E. B.

Cassatt, G. M. (New York City)

+Castle, Egerton

Ceballos, J. M. (New York)

*Chaffee, Major-General A. R.
(Washington, DC)*

+Chamberlain, H. R.

Chance, Wade

Church, Lieut A. H. (New York)

Churchill, Winston (New York)

Clemens, Samuel L. (Connecticut)

Cleveland, Hon. Grover, ex-Pres. USA
Clover, Captain Richardson, USN
Coffin, Charles A. (New York)
Coffin, William Edward (New York)
Collins, Rt. Hon. Sir R. Henn.
Colmer, Joseph G
Comings, W. R.
Cook, Samuel G. B.
Coolidge, Hon. T. J., Jr (New York)
Corbet, A. H.
Corbin, Major-General H. C.
    (Washington, DC)
Coudert, Frederic R., Jr (New York)
Crackanthorpe, M. H.
Cravath, Paul D. (New York)
Crisp, C. Birch
Crocker, W. H. (New York)
Cunard, Sir Bache E.
Cutting, R. Fulton (New York)

Darling, The Hon. Mr Justice
Davies, Julien T. (New York City)
Dean, H. Hollingsworth
+Deerhurst, Viscount
De Friese, L. H.
De Mercado, Lionel
Demorest, William Curtis (New York)
Denny, E. M.
+Depew, Hon. Chauncey M.
    (Washington, DC)
Dickinson, Hon. D. M. (Michigan)
Doran, W. S.
Doyle, Sir A. Conan
Drummond, John L.
Duke, B. N.
Duncan, A. J. M.
Duncan, William Butler (New York)
Dunlap, William A. (New York)

Eldridge, Arthur G.
Elibank, MP, The Master of
Eno, William Phelps (New York)
Evans, Hon. H. Clay (US Consul-General)

Fairbanks, R. N.
Fairchild, S. W. (New York)
Fairfax of Cameron, Lord
Farnam, Charles H., Jr
Farnham, Paulding (New York)
Feild, Thomas L.
Fife, William
Fisher, William Forbes
Fleming, Rev. Archibald
Flynn, E. F.
+Ford, I. N.
Francis, H. M. (Indiana)
Fuller, W. W. (New York)
Furness, MP, Sir Christopher

Gage, Hon. Lyman J. (Illinois)
+Gambrill, Stephen W.
Garrett, John Work.
Gibson, H. M.
Gilder, J. B.
Gilder, Richard Watson (New York City)
Gilman, Daniel C. (Indiana)
Glasgow, A. G.
Goode, R. A. J.
Goode, W. A. M.
Gorman, Hon. Arthur P. (Maryland)
Goss, E. O.
Gould, Edwin (New York)
Graves, William Leon (New York)
+Grenfell, Lt-Gen. Lord
Griffin, Gen. Eugene (New York)
Griggs, Hon. John W. (New Jersey)
Guedalla, F. M.
Guedalla, Herbert

Hall, Henry H.
Halsbury, The Earl of
Hanchett, Benton (Michigan)
Hankey, Lee (New York)
Hanson, Charles A.
Hatch, Hon. E. W. (New York)
Hatzfeldt, Prince Francois
Hay, C. Cortlandt (New York)

Hayward, T. J. (New York)
+Hay, Louis C.
Hazard, William A.
Heaton, MP, J. Henniker
Hedges, Job E. (New York)
Herrick, Hon., Myron T. (Ohio)
Hewett, G. H.
Hill, Gray
Hinkle, A. Howard (New York)
Holdich, Sir Thomas H.
Hughes, Col Herbert
Hutchinson, Arthur
+ Hutchinson, Col H. D.
Hyde, James H. (New York)

Ide, George E. (New York)
+Ingram, Herbert
Ingram, Sir William J.
Irving, Sir Henry

Jackson, George J. (New York)
James, John Sylvester (New York)
Jarvis, S. M.
Jeanne, F. A.
Jessup, Morris K. (New York)
Johnston, Edward W. (New York)
Johnston, Walter S. (New York)
Jones, Albert E. (New York)
Jones, Kennedy
Jones, Sir Alfred L.

Keene, James R. (New York)
Kennedy, Hon. Sir William Rann
Keyes, W. B.
Kimball, J. H. (Massachusetts)
Kinnaird, Lord
Knight, C. A.

Lamington, Lord
+Lambton, Rear-Admiral The Hon.
  Hedworth
Lance, Dr (New York)
Lane, John

Lawrence, Frank R. (New York)
Lee, MP, Arthur Hamilton
Leggett, Francis G. (New York)
Levis, Howard C.
Levy, Hon. Jefferson M. (New York)
Libby, W. H. (New York)
Lindsay, C. Seton
Lindsay, W. A.
Lipton, Sir Thomas
Low, A. Maurice (New York)
Lyman, Chester W. (Massachusetts)

Mabie, Hamilton W. (New York)
Mackay, Rev. D. S. (New York)
Macleod, W. M.
Macnair, J.
Macnutt, Francis A. (Rome)
Maconochie, MP, A. W.
Mahon, Col B. T.
Mahony, Roland F. (Buffalo, NY)
Mandelick, W. E.
Mansfield, Richard (New York)
Marburg, Theodore (New York)
Marburg, William A. (New York)
Martin, Bradley (New York)
Martindale, Warine B. H.
Mayer, William A. (New York)
McArthur, MP, William A.
McCall, Hon. John A. (New York)
McCall, John C. (New York)
McCook, John J. (New York)
McCormick, L. Hamilton
McCormick, The Hon. Robert
  (US Ambassador to Russia)
McCormick, Robert H., Jr (New York)
McCurdy, Richard (New York)
McCurdy, Robert H. (New York)
+McDonald, James
McDonald, J.B. (New York)
McGusty, Robert T. (New York)
McIlvaine, C. W.
McIntyre, William H. (New York)
Milburn, John G. (New York)

Milliken, E. F. (New York)
Milliken, Foster (New York)
Mitchell, Edward (New York)
Mooney, R. J. (New York)
Morton, Hon. Levi P. (New York)
Mower, George A.
Munkittrick, A.
Munsey, Frank A. (New York)
Murphy, Hon. Franklin (New York)

Napier of Magdala, Lord
+Neef, Walter
Newcastle, The Duke of
Newel, The Hon. Stanford (US Minister at The Hague)
Nicholson, Lt-Gen. Sir W. G.
Noble, Herbert (New York)
Nottingham, William (Syracuse, NY)

Ochs, Adolph S. (New York)
O'Connell, Major J. R.
O'Day, Daniel (New York)
Ogden, Robert C. (New York)
Ormiston, T. S. (New York)
Otis, Hon. Norton P. (New York)

+Parker, MP, Sir Gilbert
Parker, Percy W. (Minnesota)
Parshall, Horace Field
Parson, William E. A. (New York)
Partington, MP, O.
Patterson, R. L. (New York)
Peabody, Charles A. (New York)
Peabody, Richard A. (New York)
Pearson, C. Arthur
Peck, Ferdinand W. (Illinois)
Peddar, S. H.
Perkins, George W. (New York)
Perth, The Bishop of
Phipps, Henry
Pierce, H. Clay (New York)
Platt, Frank H. (New York)
Platt, Henry B. (New York)

Pollock, Sir Frederick
Porter, The Hon. Robert P. (New York)
Potter, Rt Rev. Henry C. (New York)
Powell, G. T.
Power, Edward H. (New York)
Priestley, MP, Arthur
Puleston, Sir John H.

Redwood, Boverton
Rice, E. Wilbur Jr (New York)
Richardson, H. D.
Richards, R. C.
+Roberts, Field Marshal Earl
Rockwell, Thomas H.
Roe, General Charles F. (New York)
Roe, Livingston, Jr
Rohl, F. R. (New York)
Roney, Ernest
Roquet, J. C. (New York)
Rosen, Walter (New York)
Rucker, Atterson W. (New York)
Rushmore, Charles E. (New York)
+Russell, Lindsay (New York)

Sanderson, Sir Percy (Consul-General, New York)
Sanger, Hon. W. Cary (New York)
Sawtelle, Captain E. M.
Schiff, Charles
Schiff, Jacob H. (New York)
Schmidlapp, J. G. (New York)
Schurman, J. G. (New York)
Seaman, Dr L. L.
Seligman, Charles D.
Seligman, Isaac N. (New York)
Sells, E. W. (New York)
Severn, G. A. (New York)
Shannon, J. J.
Shannon, Hon. Richard C. (New York)
Shiland, Andrew (New York)
Short, Edward Lyman
Siemans, Alexander
Sims, Arthur

Sinclair, John J. (New York)
+Sinclair, Ven. William McDonald
    (Archdeacon of London)
Sinderen, Howard Van (New York)
Smalley, G. W. (New York)
Smith, A. H. (New York)
Smith, H. H. Riley
Smith, Percival C. (New York)
Smith, R. A. C.
Smith, W. R.
Smith-Rewse, H. S.
Smithers, John
Snyder, Milton V. (New York)
Spalding, J. W.
Stahel, General J. (New York)
Steadman, S. F. St. J.
Stebbins, E. Vail
Stedman, Major-General Sir E.
Stern, Louis (New York)
Stern, Simon H. (New York)
Stevens, F. J.
Stevens, Marshall
Stewart, J. C. (New York)
Straight, Sir Douglas
Strathcona and Mount Royal, Lord
+Suart, Alfred

Tarbell, Gage E. (New York)
Taylor, M. F. (New York)
Temperley, Charles
Thatcher, Thomas (New York)
Thomson, C. E.
Thomson, David Croal
Tower, The Hon. Charlemagne
    (US Ambassador to Germany)
Towne, Hon. Charles A. (Minnesota)
Towne, Paul R. (New York)
Truscott, Alderman Sir G. Wyatt
Tuohy, J. M.
Turner, Major-General Sir A. E.
Turner, J. H. (Agent-General,
    British Columbia)

Underwood, F. D. (New York)

Vanderlip, F. A. (New York)

Wallace, Edward C. (New York)
Walsh, Hon. Thomas F. (Washington)
Walton, MP, J. Lawson
Walton, The Hon. Mr Justice Joseph
Ward, Count
Warfield, Edwin (Maryland)
Warren, Charles B. (Michigan)
Webb, G. Creighton (New York)
Weigall, Stanley
Wetmore, Edmund (New York)
Wheeler, General Joseph (Alabama)
White, J. G. (Washington)
Whitley, John R.
Whitridge, F. W. (New York)
Wicker, C. M. (New York)
Wilkinson, Major E. B.
Willard, Dr Sylvester
Williamson, F. Stewart (New York)
+Wilson, George T. (New York)
Wilson, J. C., Jr (New York)
Wilson, R. T. (New York)
Witham, Philip
Witherbee, F. S. (New York)
Wood, Brigadier-General L. W.
    (Washington, DC)
Woodruff, John E. (New York)
Woodward, Hon. B. D. (New York)
Woodward, Henry T.
Woodward, General Stuart L. (New York)
Wright, George
Wykes, Hunter (New York)

Yerkes, Charles T.
Young, Hon. Michael de (California)
Young, General S. B. M. (Washington, DC)

SOCIETY FUNCTIONS, 1902–2001

——— 1902 ———
8 August
Dinner for
FIELD MARSHAL EARL ROBERTS

15 October
Luncheon for
GENERALS CORBIN, YOUNG and WOOD

——— 1903 ———
3 March
Dinner for
JOSEPH CHOATE
(American ambassador 1899–1905)

19 June
Dinner for
GEORGE WYNDHAM, MP

9 July
Luncheon for
OFFICERS OF THE AMERICAN
SQUADRON

15 October
Dinner for
THE ALASKAN BOUNDARY
COMMISSION

——— 1904 ———
29 January
Supper simultaneously with
dinner in New York for
SIR MORTIMER DURAND

2 June
Luncheon for
SETH LOW

18 June
Dinner for
FIELD MARSHAL EARL ROBERTS

25 October
Dinner for
OFFICERS OF THE AMERICAN
SQUADRON

——— 1905 ———
12 April
Dinner for
HENRY CLAY EVANS
(American Consul-General)

23 June
Dinner for
WHITELAW REID
(American ambassador 1905–13)

——— 1906 ———
6 April
Dinner for
LORD CURZON

29 May
Dinner for
THE RT REV. HENRY POTTER
(Bishop of New York,
President of the Pilgrims of the United States)

——— 1907 ———
6 February
Dinner for
JAMES BRYCE
(British ambassador to Washington 1907–13)

19 April
Dinner for
THE COLONIAL PREMIERS

25 June
Luncheon for
MARK TWAIN

——— 1908 ———
12 May
Luncheon for
EDWARD ABBEY, RA

15 June
Dinner for
THE ARCHBISHOPS AND BISHOPS OF
THE PAN-AMERICAN CONGRESS

24 November
Dinner for
THE DELEGATES OF THE
INTERNATIONAL NAVAL CONFERENCE

——— 1909 ———
16 July
Luncheon for
THE AMERICAN AND BRITISH POLO TEAMS

19 November
Dinner for
J. RIDGELEY CARTER
(First Secretary, American embassy)

——— 1910 ———
9 March
Dinner for
CHARLES FAIRBANKS
(Formerly Vice-President of the United States)

10 June
Dinner for
COMMANDER ROBERT PEARY

18 November
Luncheon for
REAR-ADMIRAL J. B. MURDOCK AND
OFFICERS OF THE UNITED STATES
ATLANTIC FLEET

——— 1911 ———
23 May
Dinner for
THE PRIME MINISTERS OF THE
OVERSEAS DOMINIONS

28 June
Dinner for
JOHN HAYS HAMMOND
(Special ambassador from the United States to
the coronation of King George V)

——— 1912 ———
15 March
Dinner for
ERNEST THOMPSON SETON

3 May
Dinner for
DR W. T. GRENFELL

24 June
Dinner
TO CELEBRATE THE TENTH
ANNIVERSARY

15 November
Luncheon for
WILLIAM PHILLIPS
(First Secretary, American embassy)

——— 1913 ———
6 June
Dinner for
WALTER HINES PAGE
(American ambassador 1913–18)

6 November
Dinner for
JAMES BRYCE
(British ambassador to Washington 1907–13)

——— 1914 ———
24 April
Dinner for
SIR ERNEST SHACKLETON

2 July
Luncheon for
LORD WIMBORNE AND THE BRITISH
POLO TEAM

31 July
Luncheon for
HARRY BRITTAIN

──────── 1915 ────────
15 April
50TH ANNIVERSARY OF THE DEATH OF
ABRAHAM LINCOLN
(Address by Sir Gilbert Parker, MP)

30 June
Address on "The Present Phase of the War"
HILAIRE BELLOC

20 July
Address on "The Naval War"
A. H. POLLEN
(Naval journalist, author of *The Navy in Battle*, 1918)

──────── 1916 ────────
26 January
Address on "Life in Belgium"
MAÎTRE GASTON DE LEVAL
(Adviser to the United States Legation in Brussels)

17 March
Address on "Australia and the War"
W. M. HUGHES
(Prime Minister of Australia)

5 July
Luncheon for
JAMES BECK
(Assistant Attorney-General of
the United States)

25 October
Address on "New Zealand and the War"
W. F. MASSEY
(Prime Minister of New Zealand)

──────── 1917 ────────
12 April
Dinner
TO MARK THE ENTRY OF THE UNITED
STATES INTO THE WAR

──────── 1918 ────────
25 June
Dinner
following the Annual Meeting

12 July
Luncheon for
W. M. HUGHES
(Prime Minister of Australia)

28 November
Luncheon
TO CELEBRATE THANKSGIVING DAY

──────── 1919 ────────
10 January
Luncheon for
JOHN DAVIS
(American ambassador 1918–21)

21 March
Dinner for
ADMIRAL WILLIAM SIMS

──────── 1920 ────────
21 January
Dinner for
THE PRINCE OF WALES

15 March
Dinner for
SIR AUCKLAND GEDDES
(British ambassador to
Washington 1920–4)

29 April
Luncheon for
GENERAL CHARLES SHERRILL
(Chairman of the Pilgrims of
the United States)

1 June
Luncheon for
HUNTER WYKES
(Secretary of the Pilgrims of
the United States)

11 October
Luncheon for
REAR-ADMIRAL A. P. NIBLACK

18 November
House dinner

31 December
Dinner for
THE CORNELL UNIVERSITY CROSS-
COUNTRY TEAM

———— 1921 ————
20 January
Luncheon for
REAR-ADMIRAL A. P. NIBLACK

28 February
Dinner for
JOHN DAVIS
(American ambassador 1918–21)

19 May
Dinner for
GEORGE HARVEY
(American ambassador 1921–3)

26 May
Luncheon for
ADMIRAL WILLIAM SIMS

28 June
Dinner for
THE UNITED STATES POLO TEAM

17 October
Dinner for
J. BUTLER WRIGHT
(Counselor, American embassy)

31 October
Dinner for
THE BRITISH DELEGATES TO THE
WASHINGTON CONFERENCE

———— 1922 ————
20 February
Dinner for
ARTHUR BALFOUR, MP
(On the return of the delegates to the
Washington conference)

3 April
Luncheon for
ARTHUR TWINING HADLEY
(President Emeritus of Yale University)

7 June
Dinner for
JAMES BECK
(Solicitor-General of the United States)

19 June
Dinner for
WILLIAM TAFT
(Chief Justice of the United States)

12 July
Dinner for
SIR AUCKLAND GEDDES
(British ambassador to Washington 1920–4)

14 December
Luncheon for
THE AMERICAN COMMISSION FOR
ADJUSTMENT OF FOREIGN CLAIMS

———— 1923 ————
28 February
Dinner for
STANLEY BALDWIN, MP
(Chancellor of the Exchequer)

14 May
Luncheon for
THE AMERICAN GOLFERS

15 June
Dinner for
DR NICHOLAS MURRAY BUTLER
(President of Columbia University)

11 July
Dinner for
ALBERT D. LASKER
(retiring chairman of the US Shipping Board)
and the official party arriving by the *Leviathan*
marking the first transatlantic voyage under
United States Lines management

21 July
Dinner for
THE HARVARD AND YALE ATHLETIC
TEAMS AND THE AMERICAN FENCERS

23 October
Dinner for
GEORGE HARVEY
(American ambassador 1921–3)

————— 1924 —————
1 February
Dinner for
FRANK KELLOGG
(American ambassador 1923–5)
and
SIR ESME HOWARD
(British ambassador to Washington 1924–30)

6 March
Dinner for
SIR AUCKLAND GEDDES
(British ambassador to Washington 1920–4)

7 May
Luncheon for
MAJOR SOLBERT
(Military attaché, American embassy)

21 July
Dinner for
CHARLES EVANS HUGHES
(Secretary of State of the United States)

9 October
Dinner for
ROBERT SKINNER
(American Consul-General 1914–24))
and LEE WASHINGTON
(American Consul-General 1924–8)

————— 1925 —————
30 January
Dinner for
FRANK KELLOGG
(American ambassador 1923–5)

4 May
Dinner for
ALANSON HOUGHTON
(American ambassador 1925–9)

11 May
Luncheon for
SIR ROBERT FALCONER
(President of Toronto University)

4 June
Dinner for
THE AMERICAN DOCTORS

6 October
Luncheon for
DR ROBERT McELROY
(Harmsworth Professor of American History at
Oxford University)

————— 1926 —————
28 April
Dinner for
THE MARQUESS OF READING
(Viceroy and Governor-General of India 1921–6)

4 June
Luncheon for
THE 107TH INFANTRY, UNITED STATES ARMY

12 July
Dinner for
THE PRINCETON AND CORNELL
UNIVERSITIES ATHLETIC TEAMS

26 October
Dinner for
THE FOOTBALL TEAM FROM
WORCESTER, MASSACHUSETTS

1 December
Dinner for
THE DUKE OF YORK

——— 1927 ———

18 May
Dinner for
SIR ROBERT BORDEN
(Prime Minister of Canada 1911–20; Rhodes
lecturer 1927)

30 June
Dinner for
ADMIRAL GUY BURRAGE AND OFFICERS
OF THE US FLAGSHIP *DETROIT*

12 July
Dinner for
THE RT REV. WILLIAM MANNING
(Bishop of New York)

26 July
Dinner for
THE AMERICAN EDITORS

——— 1928 ———

29 March
Luncheon for
E. H. SIMMONS
(President of the New York Stock Exchange)

17 May
Dinner for
TIMOTHY HEALY
(Governor-General of the Irish Free State
1922–7)

11 June
Dinner for
ADMIRAL GUY BURRAGE AND OFFICERS
OF THE US FLAGSHIP *DETROIT*

18 July
Luncheon for
BOYLSTON BEAL
(Honorary Counselor of the American
embassy)

7 November
Luncheon for
ALBERT HALSTEAD
(American Consul-General 1928–32)

5 December
Dinner
TO CELEBRATE THE SIGNING OF THE
PACT FOR THE RENUNCIATION OF WAR

14 December
Dinner for
R. D. BLUMENFELD
(President of the Institute of Journalists)

——— 1929 ———

26 March
Dinner for
ALANSON HOUGHTON
(American ambassador 1925–9)

8 May
Dinner for
CHARLES EVANS HUGHES
(Chief Justice of the United States)

18 June
Dinner for
GENERAL CHARLES DAWES
(American ambassador 1929–32)

25 June
Luncheon for
THE COLUMBIA UNIVERSITY
ROWING TEAM

19 September
Dinner for
THE FOOTBALL TEAM FROM
WORCESTER, MASSACHUSETTS

22 November
Dinner for
FRANK KELLOGG
(Secretary of State of the United States
1925–9)

17 December
Luncheon for
THE EARL OF DERBY
(Chairman of the Pilgrims 1929–45)

——— 1930 ———

28 January
Dinner for
THE DELEGATES TO THE LONDON
NAVAL CONFERENCE

12 February
Dinner for
LORD DESBOROUGH
(Chairman of the Pilgrims 1919–29)

4 March
Dinner for
SIR ESME HOWARD
(British ambassador to Washington
1924–30)

15 May
Dinner for
DR NICHOLAS MURRAY BUTLER
(President of the Pilgrims of the United States)

——— 1931 ———

17 February
Luncheon for
SIR HARRY GLOSTER ARMSTRONG
(British Consul-General in New York
1920–31)

4 March
Dinner for
THE EARL OF WILLINGDON
(Viceroy-designate of India and retiring
Governor-General of Canada)

29 May
Luncheon for
FREDERICK KEPPEL
(President of the Carnegie Corporation)
and
HENRY ZALLO
(President of the Carnegie Foundation)
and
HENRY JAMES

24 June
Luncheon for
EDWARD HARKNESS
(Founder of the Pilgrim Trust)

18 July
Dinner for
THE HARVARD AND YALE
UNIVERSITIES ATHLETIC TEAMS

——— 1932 ———

1 March
Luncheon for
DWIGHT DAVIS
(Minister of War of the United States 1925–9;
founder of the Davis Cup competition)

14 April
Dinner for
ANDREW MELLON
(American ambassador 1932–3)

10 May
Luncheon for
PROFESSOR GEORGE LYMAN
KITTREDGE
(Professor of English, Harvard University)

12 July
Dinner
TO CELEBRATE THE BICENTENARY OF
THE BIRTH OF GEORGE WASHINGTON

18 October
Luncheon for
ALBERT HALSTEAD
(American Consul-General 1928–32)

22 November
Luncheon for
ROBERT FRAZER
(American Consul-General 1932–7)

——— 1933 ———

21 February
Dinner for
ANDREW MELLON
(American ambassador 1932–3)

16 May
Dinner for
RAMSAY MacDONALD, MP
(Prime Minister)

30 May
Dinner for
ROBERT WORTH BINGHAM
(American ambassador 1933–8)

27 June
Luncheon for
CORDELL HULL
(Secretary of State of the United States)

——— 1934 ———
2 May
Luncheon for
CASS GILBERT
(Member of the Executive Committee of the
Pilgrims of the United States)

3 July
Dinner for
DR NICHOLAS MURRAY BUTLER
(President of the Pilgrims of the United States)

21 July
Dinner for
THE PRINCETON AND CORNELL
UNIVERSITIES ATHLETIC TEAMS

10 October
Dinner for
TOM SOPWITH AND THE CREW OF THE
ENDEAVOUR

——— 1935 ———
30 April
Dinner for
THE DUKE OF KENT

12 July
Luncheon for
JAMES GERARD
(Vice-President of the Pilgrims of the
United States)

20 July
Dinner for
THE HARVARD AND YALE UNIVERSITIES
ATHLETIC TEAMS

20 November
Dinner for
JOHN FINLEY
(Associate Editor of the *New York Times*)

19 December
Dinner for
THE DELEGATES TO THE LONDON
NAVAL CONFERENCE

——— 1936 ———
13 January
Luncheon for
WILLIAM PHILLIPS
(Under-Secretary of State of the
United States)

14 July
Luncheon for
THE RT REV. JAMES DE WOLF PERRY
(Presiding Bishop of the Episcopalian Church
of the United States)

23 July
Luncheon for
DANIEL ROPER
(Secretary of Commerce of the United States)
and
WILLIAM ALEXANDER JULIAN
(Treasurer of the United States)

15 August
Dinner for
THE OLYMPIC GAMES TEAMS OF THE
UNITED STATES AND GREAT BRITAIN

26 November
Luncheon for
JAMES FARLEY
(Postmaster-General of the United States)

——— 1937 ———

19 May
Dinner for
JAMES GERARD
(Special ambassador from the United States
to the coronation of King George VI)

5 October
Luncheon for
ROBERT FRAZER
(American Consul-General 1932–7)

——— 1938 ———

18 March
Dinner for
JOSEPH KENNEDY
(American ambassador 1938–41)

18 July
Luncheon for
JOHN DAVIS
(American ambassador 1918–21)

23 July
Dinner for
THE PRINCETON AND CORNELL
UNIVERSITIES ATHLETIC TEAMS

——— 1939 ———

7 March
Luncheon for
FRANK HOGAN
(President of the American Bar Association)

13 July
Dinner for
THE MARQUESS OF LOTHIAN
(British ambassador to Washington 1939–40)

17 July
Luncheon for
DOUGLAS JENKINS
(American Consul-General 1937–9)

——— 1941 ———

9 January
Luncheon for
VISCOUNT HALIFAX
(British ambassador to Washington 1941–6)

18 March
Luncheon for
JOHN WINANT
(American ambassador 1941–6)

——— 1942 ———

6 May
Reception
TO CELEBRATE THE 40TH
ANNIVERSARY OF THE PILGRIMS

——— 1943 ———

16 September
Luncheon for
FIELD MARSHAL VISCOUNT WAVELL
(Viceroy and Governor-General of India
1943–7)

——— 1945 ———

5 December
Dinner for
CLEMENT ATTLEE
(Prime Minister)

——— 1946 ———

4 February
Dinner for
MRS ELEANOR ROOSEVELT
(United States Delegate to the United
Nations Organisation)

30 April
Dinner for
JOHN WINANT
(American ambassador 1941–6)
and
LORD INVERCHAPEL
(British ambassador to Washington 1946–8)

28 May
Dinner for
AVERELL HARRIMAN
(American ambassador 1946–7)
and
THE EARL OF HALIFAX
(British ambassador to Washington 1941–6)

———— 1947 ————
22 April
Dinner for
LEWIS DOUGLAS
(American ambassador 1947–50)

12 December
Dinner for
GEORGE MARSHALL
(Secretary of State of the United States)

———— 1948 ————
12 April
Dinner for
MRS ELEANOR ROOSEVELT
on the occasion of the unveiling of the
Roosevelt Memorial

24 November
Luncheon for
SIR FRANCIS EVANS
(British Consul-General in New York)

———— 1949 ————
23 May
Luncheon for
WINTHROP ALDRICH
(Chairman of the Chase National Bank of New York)

16 June
Dinner for
THOMAS FINLETTER
(United States Minister in charge of Economic Co-
operation Administration in the United Kingdom)

12 July
Luncheon for
ADMIRAL RICHARD CONOLLY
(Commander-in-Chief, United States Naval
Forces Eastern Atlantic and Mediterranean)

———— 1950 ————
4 April
Dinner for
JOHN McCLOY
(American High Commissioner for Germany)

10 May
Dinner for
DEAN ACHESON
(Secretary of State of the United States)

26 June
Luncheon for
JOHN DAVIS
(President of the Pilgrims of the United States)

6 November
Dinner for
LEWIS DOUGLAS
(American ambassador 1947–50)

———— 1951 ————
9 January
Dinner for
WALTER GIFFORD
(American ambassador 1950–3)

———— 1952 ————
18 March
Luncheon for
DR JAMES CONANT
(President of Harvard University)

18 June
Dinner for
ANTHONY EDEN
(Secretary of State for Foreign Affairs)

14 October
Dinner for
GENERAL MATTHEW RIDGWAY
(Supreme Commander Allied Powers in
Europe)

16 December
Dinner for
SIR OLIVER FRANKS
(British ambassador to Washington 1948–52)

———— 1953 ————

21 January
Dinner for
WALTER GIFFORD
(American ambassador 1950–3)

19 March
Dinner for
WINTHROP ALDRICH
(American ambassador 1953–7)
and
TO CELEBRATE THE FIFTY YEARS

———— 1954 ————

12 January
Luncheon for
WALTON BUTTERWORTH
(American Minister 1953–5)

18 March
Dinner for
SIR GLADWYN JEBB
(United Kingdom Permanent Representative
to the United Nations 1950–4)
and
DAG HAMMARSKJÖLD
(Secretary-General of the United Nations)

16 November
Dinner for
DR GEOFFREY FISHER
(Archbishop of Canterbury)

———— 1955 ————

20 July
Luncheon for
DR A. WHITNEY GRISWOLD
(President of Yale University)

1 November
Dinner for
HAROLD STASSEN
(Special Assistant to the President of the
United States for Disarmament)

———— 1956 ————

21 June
Dinner for
HARRY TRUMAN
(President of the United States 1945–53)

9 October
Luncheon for
THOMAS STANLEY
(Governor of Virginia and Chairman of the
Virginia 350th Anniversary Commission)

———— 1957 ————

31 January
Dinner for
WINTHROP ALDRICH
(American ambassador 1953–7)

4 April
Dinner for
JOHN HAY WHITNEY
(American ambassador 1957–61)

———— 1958 ————

23 October
Committee Dinner for
SIR CAMPBELL STUART
(Chairman 1948–58)

25 November
Luncheon for
RICHARD NIXON
(Vice-President of the United States)

———— 1959 ————

5 May
Dinner for
EUGENE BLACK
(President of the International Bank for
Reconstruction and Development)

———— 1960 ————

8 April
Luncheon for
HUGH BULLOCK
(President of the Pilgrims of the United States)

——— 1961 ———

11 January
Dinner for
JOHN HAY WHITNEY
(American ambassador 1957–61)

2 May
Dinner for
DAVID BRUCE
(American ambassador 1961–9)

18 July
Dinner for
DAVID ORMSBY GORE
(British ambassador to Washington 1961–5)

——— 1962 ———

10 January
Dinner for
SIR HAROLD CACCIA
(British ambassador to Washington 1956–61)

14 August
Luncheon for
GENERAL DWIGHT D. EISENHOWER
(President of the United States 1953–61)

——— 1963 ———

9 December
Dinner for
JOHN McCLOY
(Chairman of the Ford Foundation)

——— 1964 ———

28 January
Dinner for
AIR MARSHAL SIR THOMAS PIKE
(Deputy Supreme Allied Commander Europe)
(Replacing General Lyman Lemnitzer, United
States Army, Supreme Allied Commander
Europe, unable to be present because of
urgent military duties in Cyprus)

23 November
Dinner for
ALISTAIR COOKE

——— 1965 ———

29 March
Dinner for
SIR PATRICK DEAN
(British ambassador to Washington
1965–8)

29 November
Dinner for
GEORGE WOODS
(President of the World Bank)

——— 1966 ———

4 March
Dinner for
ARTHUR GOLDBERG
(Permanent Representative of the
United States to the
United Nations)

——— 1967 ———

27 June
Dinner for
SENATOR JACOB JAVITS
(United States Senator from New York)

1 October
Afternoon party at
Hever Castle

——— 1968 ———

24 October
Luncheon for
ROY JENKINS, MP
(Chancellor of the Exchequer)

2 December
Dinner for
JOHN FREEMAN
(British ambassador to Washington
1968–71)

——— 1969 ———

18 February
Dinner for
DAVID BRUCE
(American ambassador 1961–9)

1 May
Luncheon for
HUBERT HUMPHREY
(Director of the
Encyclopedia Britannica)
and
SENATOR WILLIAM BENTON
(Chairman of the
Encyclopedia Britannica)

28 May
Dinner for
WALTER ANNENBERG
(American ambassador 1969–74)

4 December
Reception at the Middle Temple

——— 1970 ———

5 February
Dinner for
GENERAL ANDREW GOODPASTER,
United States Army
(Supreme Allied Commander Europe)

25 February
Luncheon for
LEONARD BERNSTEIN

30 June
Reception at Winfield House

8 December
Dinner for
THE PRINCE OF WALES

——— 1971 ———

11 January
Dinner for
THE EARL OF CROMER
(British ambassador to Washington 1971–4)

4 October
Dinner for
THE MEMBERS OF THE AMERICAN
EMBASSY AND THEIR LADIES

——— 1972 ———

25 January
Dinner
TO CELEBRATE THE 70TH ANNIVERSARY

5 June
Luncheon for
HUGH BULLOCK
(President of the Pilgrims of the
United States)

5 July
Reception at St James's Palace

13 July
Reception and Private View of the Armand
Hammer Collection at the Royal Academy

30 November
"Dining In" Night for
MEMBERS AND THEIR LADIES

——— 1973 ———

15 October
Dinner for
ADMIRAL WORTH BAGLEY
(Commander-in-Chief, United States Naval
Forces Europe)

4 December
Reception at the Banqueting House, Whitehall

12 December
Dinner for
HENRY KISSINGER
(Secretary of State of the United States)

——— 1974 ———

6 February
Dinner for
SIR PETER RAMSBOTHAM
(British ambassador to Washington 1974–7)

14 March
Dinner at the Mansion House for
SIR HUGH WONTNER
(Lord Mayor of London)

10 June
Dinner for
WALTER ANNENBERG
(American ambassador 1969–74)
and
THE EARL OF CROMER
(British ambassador to Washington 1971–4)

20 June
Reception at the House of Lords

4 September
Luncheon for
MAYOR TOM BRADLEY
(Mayor of Los Angeles)

11 November
Dinner for
SENATOR HENRY JACKSON
(United States Senator from Washington)

——— 1975 ———

11 March
Dinner for
ELLIOTT RICHARDSON
(American ambassador 1975–6)

7 April
Dinner for
RONALD REAGAN
(Governor of California 1967–74)

20 October
Dinner for
GENERAL ALEXANDER HAIG,
United States Army
(Supreme Allied Commander Europe)

——— 1976 ———

9 February
Dinner for
EDWARD HEATH, MP

31 March
Dinner for
MRS ANNE ARMSTRONG
(American ambassador 1976–7)

6 July
Dinner for
THE QUEEN MOTHER
to celebrate the American Bicentenary

13 July
Reception and preview of
"American Art: 1750–1800.
Towards Independence"
at the Victoria and Albert Museum

4 October
Reception at the Savoy for those who worked on
the exhibition at the Victoria and Albert Museum

——— 1977 ———

14 February
Luncheon for
MRS ANNE ARMSTRONG
(American ambassador 1976–7)

15 June
Dinner for
KINGMAN BREWSTER
(American ambassador 1977–81)

——— 1978 ———

13 March
Dinner for
DAVID OWEN, MP
(Secretary of State for Foreign and
Commonwealth Affairs)

6 April
Reception at St James's Palace in honour of
THE QUEEN MOTHER

2 October
Reception at Gray's Inn Hall for
SIR PETER RAMSBOTHAM
(British ambassador to Washington 1974–7)

29 November
Dinner at Goldsmiths' Hall for
JAMES SCHLESINGER
(Secretary of Energy of the United States)

——— 1979 ———
17 January
Reception at Lambeth Palace

21 March
Reception at St James's Palace in honour of
THE QUEEN AND PRINCE PHILIP

9 July
Reception at Fishmongers' Hall for
SIR NICHOLAS HENDERSON
(British ambassador to Washington 1979–82)

November
Dinner at the Plaisterers Hall for
H. E. TAPLEY BENNETT
(United States ambassador to NATO)
and
GENERAL BERNARD ROGERS,
United States Army
(Supreme Allied Commander Europe)

——— 1980 ———
29 May
Reception at Apsley House

25 June
Luncheon for
SHIRLEY HUFSTEDLER
(Secretary of Education of the United States)

1 July
Buffet supper at Hever Castle
following the Annual Meeting

——— 1981 ———
29 January
Dinner for
MRS MARGARET THATCHER, MP
(Prime Minister)

20 February
Reception at Goldsmiths' Hall for
KINGMAN BREWSTER
(American ambassador 1977–81)

26 May
Dinner for
JOHN LOUIS
(American ambassador 1981–3)

6 July
Reception at Goldsmiths' Hall

12 October
Reception at the American embassy for
EUGENE ROSTOW
(Director of the United States Arms Control
and Disarmament Agency)

——— 1982 ———
23 February
Luncheon for
SENATOR JOHN TOWERS
(Chairman of the United States Senate
American Services Committee)

12 July
Dinner for
FRANCIS PYM, MP
(Secretary of State for Foreign and
Commonwealth Affairs)

25 October
Dinner for
SIR NICHOLAS HENDERSON
(British ambassador to Washington 1979–82)
and
SIR ANTHONY PARSONS
(Permanent Representative of the United
Kingdom to the United Nations)

——— 1983 ———

21 June
Dinner for
CASPAR WEINBERGER
(Secretary of Defense of the United States)

11 July
Dinner for
GEORGE THOMAS
to mark his retirement as Speaker of
the House of Commons

24 October
US Navy Command brief, given by
ADMIRAL HOLCOMB
(Deputy Commander-in-Chief, United States
Naval Forces Europe)

26 October
Reception at Gray's Inn for
JOHN LOUIS
(American ambassador 1981–3)

1 November
Luncheon for
LORD ASTOR OF HEVER
(Chairman 1967–7; president 1977–83)

——— 1984 ———

16 January
Dinner for
CHARLES PRICE
(American ambassador 1984–9)

17 July
Dinner for
WARREN BURGER
(Chief Justice of the United States)

8 November
Royal Navy briefing
at Admiralty House

——— 1985 ———

2 May
Reception at the Imperial War Museum
to commemorate Victory in Europe 1945

10 December
Luncheon for
GEORGE SCHULTZ
(Secretary of State of the United States)

——— 1986 ———

13 February
Dinner for
SIR GEOFFREY HOWE, MP
(Secretary of State for Foreign and
Commonwealth Affairs)

10 July
Dinner for
SIR ANTHONY ACLAND
(British ambassador to Washington 1986–91)

13 October
Reception at Gray's Inn for
SIR OLIVER WRIGHT
(British ambassador to Washington 1983–6)

——— 1987 ———

22 September
Reception at the House of Lords

18 November
Dinner for
GENERAL JOHN GALVIN
(Supreme Allied Commander Europe)

——— 1988 ———

21 January
Dinner for
HENRY KISSINGER
(Secretary of State of the United States 1973–7)

23 March
Dinner for
VERNON WALTERS
(United States Permanent Representative to
the United Nations)

26 September
Reception at Winfield House

——— 1989 ———
12 January
Dinner for
CHARLES PRICE
(American ambassador 1984–9)

18 May
Dinner for
HENRY CATTO
(American ambassador 1989–91)

——— 1990 ———
18 July
Dinner for
DOUGLAS HURD, MP
(Secretary of State for Foreign and
Commonwealth Affairs)

28 November
Luncheon at the Royal Overseas League for
THE HOUSE OF REPRESENTATIVES
COMMITTEE ON FOREIGN AFFAIRS

——— 1991 ———
17 April
Reception at the Bank of England

4 July
Dinner for
RAYMOND SEITZ
(American ambassador 1991–4)

23 September
Lecture: "The Future of Higher Education" by
JOHN ASHWORTH
(Director of the
London School of Economics)
following the Annual Meeting
at the American embassy

21 October
Dinner for
SIR ROBIN RENWICK
(British ambassador to Washington 1991–5)

25 November
Dinner for
JASON MCMANUS
(Editor of *Time Life*)

——— 1992 ———
5 May
Reception and private view of "Rembrandt:
The Master and his Workshop"
at the National Gallery

21 September
Reception and lecture on the American
election by
PROFESSOR NELSON POLSBY
at the English-Speaking Union
(Jointly with the English-Speaking Union)

23 November
Lecture: "Europe and America:
Post Maastricht" by
JOHN DREW
(Head of the European Community Offices)

——— 1993 ———
9 February
Reception and lecture by
JEREMY ISAACS
at the Royal Opera House

15 March
Reception at Christie's

4 May
Reception at Winfield House

20 September
Lecture:
"The Reinvention of Government" by
SIR ROBIN BUTLER
(Secretary of the Cabinet
and Head of the Home Civil Service)
following the Annual Meeting
at the American embassy

——— 1994 ———

27 January
Dinner at the Mansion House for
CASPAR WEINBERGER
(Chairman of *Forbes* Magazine; Secretary of
Defense of the United States 1981–7)

3 February
Committee dinner for
ROBERT SIGMON
(Chairman 1977–93)

1 March
Luncheon for
DAVID AARON
(United States representative to the OECD
in Paris)

19 April
Dinner for
RAYMOND SEITZ
(American ambassador 1991–4)

3 May
Reception at the House of Commons

22 June
Reception at St James's Palace in honour of
THE QUEEN

28 July
Dinner for
ADMIRAL WILLIAM CROWE
(American ambassador 1994–7)

19 September
Sir Harry Brittain Lecture by
ROBERT HUNTER
following the Annual Meeting at the
American embassy

15 November
Dinner for
MALCOLM RIFKIND, MP
(Secretary of State for Defence)

——— 1995 ———

15 February
Dinner for
KENNETH CLARKE, MP
(Chancellor of the Exchequer)

27 March
Luncheon for
RICHARD GARDNER
(American ambassador to Spain)

12 April
COMMEMORATION OF THE 50TH
ANNIVERSARY OF THE UNVEILING OF
THE STATUE OF
FRANKLIN D. ROOSEVELT

2 May
Reception at Winfield House

17 July
Dinner at the Middle Temple for
WILLIAM REHNQUIST
(Chief Justice of the United States)

25 September
Sir Harry Brittain Lecture by
SIR CRISPIN TICKELL
following the Annual Meeting at the
American embassy

9 November
Luncheon for
SIR ROBIN RENWICK
(British ambassador to Washington 1991–5)

——— 1996 ———

12 February
Reflections Lecture by
LORD SHERFIELD

12 March
Reception and lecture on the
American elections by
PROFESSOR SEYMOUR MARTIN LIPSET
at the English-Speaking Union
(Joint Pilgrims and ESU event)

25 March
Dinner for
PETER SUTHERLAND
(Chairman of Goldman Sachs International)

8 May
Reception and visit to the
Royal Botanic Gardens, Kew

9 September
Sir Harry Brittain Lecture by
DAME STELLA RIMINGTON
following the Annual Meeting at the
American embassy

18 November
Dinner for
FIELD MARSHAL SIR PETER INGE
(Chief of the Defence Staff)

———— 1997 ————
12 March
Supper and concert: "An Evening with Stilgoe
and Skellern" at the South Bank

24 March
Reflections Lecture by
FIELD MARSHAL THE LORD BRAMALL

7 May
Reception at the House of Commons

27 August
Luncheon for
THE UNITED STATES SENATE
DELEGATION TO THE MEETING OF
THE BRITISH-AMERICAN
PARLIAMENTARY GROUP

9 September
Luncheon for
ADMIRAL WILLIAM CROWE
(American ambassador 1994–7)

22 September
Sir Harry Brittain Lecture by
SIR CHRISTOPHER BLAND
following the Annual Meeting at the
American embassy

20 October
Dinner for
JOHN MAJOR, MP
(Former Prime Minister)

18 November
Dinner for
PHILIP LADER
(American ambassador 1997–2001)

———— 1998 ————
18 February
Luncheon for
SIR JOHN KERR
(British ambassador to Washington 1995–7)

29 April
Reception and concert of American music at
the Barbican

18 May
Dinner at the Middle Temple for
SANDRA DAY O'CONNOR
(Justice of the Supreme Court
of the United States)

21 September
Sir Harry Brittain Lecture by
LORD PUTTNAM
following the Annual Meeting at the
American embassy

17 November
Luncheon at the Reform Club for
SIR JOHN WESTON
(British Permanent Representative to the
United Nations 1995–8)

———— 1999 ————
10 March
Reflections Lecture by
LORD HEALEY

17 March
Luncheon for
BARONESS SYMONS OF DEAN
(Parliamentary Under-Secretary of State,
Foreign and Commonwealth Office)

30 June
Dinner for
GEORGE ROBERTSON, MP
(Secretary of State for Defence)

20 September
Sir Harry Brittain Lecture by
FELIX ROHATYN
following the Annual Meeting at the
American embassy

6 October
Dinner at the Middle Temple for
LORD BINGHAM OF CORNHILL
(Lord Chief Justice)

———— 2000 ————

10 February
Dinner for
PROFESSOR ANTHONY GIDDENS
(Director of the London School of
Economics)

15 March
Buffet lunch and talk by
MICHAEL KAISER
at the Royal Opera House

12 April
Luncheon and talk by
JONATHAN FREEDLAND
(author of *Bring Home the Revolution – The
Case for a British Republic*)

8 May
Reception at Winfield House

16 June
Lunch and visit to the National Maritime
Museum, Greenwich

25 September
Sir Harry Brittain Lecture by
SIR ROBERT MAY
following the Annual Meeting at the
American embassy

10 October
Panel discussion: "New Millennium: New
American Elections"

29 November
Dinner for
MICHAEL HESELTINE, MP
(Former Deputy Prime Minister)

12 December
Reception at the
Foreign and Commonwealth Office
(Jointly with the British-American Project)

———— 2001 ————

8 February
Reflections Lecture by
SIR MARTIN JACOMB

26 February
Dinner for
PHILIP LADER
(American ambassador 1997–2001)

16 May
Dinner for
GENERAL SIR CHARLES GUTHRIE
[Now Lord Guthrie]

24 September
Sir Harry Brittain Lecture by
SIR JOHN STEVENS
following the Annual Meeting at the
American embassy

2 October
Exhibition of work by Brendan Hansbro
at the Curwen Gallery, London

16 October
Dinner for
WILLIAM FARISH
(American ambassador 2001–)

19 November
Luncheon and talk by
PROFESSOR DAVID CANNADINE
at the English-Speaking Union

PICTURE CREDITS

Illustrations are listed by page number, and have been reproduced by permission of the copyright holders or sources shown. In a few cases, efforts to trace the copyright holder have been unsuccessful. Any omissions or errors of attribution that are brought to the attention of the publisher will be corrected in future editions. Illustrations not credited here are the property of and reproduced by permission of the Pilgrims Society.

By permission of the Warden and Fellows of All Souls College, Oxford: 31 (detail), 63 bottom

Alpha Photographic (Sport and General): 29 bottom (detail), 120 top, 122 top, 128 top, 128 bottom, 134 top, 138 top, 160 top (also by courtesy of The Savoy Group)

Associated Press: 24 (detail), 26 (detail), 27 top (detail), 27 bottom (detail), 42 top (detail), 42 bottom (detail), 120 bottom, 122 bottom, 125 top, 126 top (also by courtesy of The Savoy Group), 129 top, 136 top, 147 bottom, 148 top, 149 top, 150 bottom, 153 top, 153 bottom left, 154 bottom, 156 top, 157 top, 159 top, 165 top

Astonleigh Studio: 154 top

Lord Astor: 39 top (detail), 65 centre (photo by Bridget Astor)

Atlantic Syndication (*Daily Mail*): 139 top, 152 top

Baron Photo Centre: 29 top (detail), 30 bottom (detail), 63 top, 68 top, 127, 132 bottom

Bill Bates – Van Hallan: 41 centre (detail), 46 top (detail), 46 bottom (detail), 163 bottom, 164 top, 164 bottom, 165 bottom, 166 bottom, 167 top, 167 bottom, 168 top, 169 top, 169 bottom, 170 top, 170 bottom, 171 top, 171 bottom, 172 top

S. and C. Calman: 173 top

Central News Agency: 25 (detail), 112 top, 115 bottom, 116 top

Central Press Photos: 130 top

Terry Chambers: ii (frontispiece)

Corbis/UPI: 151 bottom, 158 bottom

Daily Graphic Picture Services: 139 centre

Daily Telegraph: 42 centre (detail), 155 top

Lord Derby: 21 bottom (detail), 104 bottom, 119 bottom, 124 top

Viscount Gage (photography by Edward Reeves): 21 top (detail), 67 bottom

Lord Halifax: 145 bottom

Hulton Getty (Keystone): 123 bottom, 132 top, 135 top, 137 bottom left, 142 top

Illustrated London News Picture Library: 15 (detail), 66, 67 top, 79, 85, 107, 113, 121 bottom

Andy Lane: 48 bottom (detail), 174 top

Patricia Makins: 48 top (detail), 174 bottom

By courtesy of the National Portrait Gallery, London: 12 (detail), 18 (detail), 36 top (detail), 37 (detail), 60, 61 top, 62, 64 top, 64 bottom, 70 bottom, 87 left

New York Times Photos: 137 top

News International (*Times*): 36 bottom (detail), 44 bottom (detail), 68 bottom, 131, 144 bottom, 148 bottom, 149 bottom, 163 top

News Photos: 121 top left

Photographic Agency Darley: 110 top, 111 top
Photographic News Agencies, 136 top
Pilgrim Trust: 118 bottom
Pilgrims Society (photography by Ken Adlard): 13 (detail), 16 (detail), 72, 73, 84, 99 top, 106, 108–9, 134–5
Planet News: 30 top (detail), 130 bottom, 138 bottom
Press Association: 33 (detail), 34 (detail), 35 (detail), 38 (detail), 39 bottom (detail), 65 top, 133 top, 133 inset, 133 bottom, 134 top, 140 top, 140 bottom, 141 top, 141 bottom, 145 top, 147 top, 150 top, 152 bottom
The Royal Collection © 2000. Her Majesty Queen Elizabeth II: 19 (detail), 61 bottom
Reproduced by courtesy of The Savoy Group: 41 bottom (detail), 83, 126 top, 156 bottom left (photography by Brian Worth), 160 top, 162 top, 162 bottom
Gerald G. Sharp: 49 (detail), 173 bottom
The Society of Authors, literary representative of the Estate of John Masefield: 103
Sulgrave Manor Board: 100
Swaebe: 153 bottom right
W. G. Tasker: 142 centre
Topical Press Agency: 22 (detail), 105 top, 111 top, 114 top
Underwood & Underwood: 112 bottom
Van Hallan: 41 top (detail), 158 top, 159 bottom, 160 bottom, 161 top, 161 bottom, 162 top (also by courtesy of The Savoy Group)
By permission of A. P. Watt Ltd on behalf of the National Trust for Places of Historical Interest or Natural Beauty: 119 top

INDEX

n followed by a numeral indicates a numbered note on pages 52–8.
For example, *57n67* indicates note 67 on page 57.